THE BURNINGS
1920

PEARSE LAWLOR

MERCIER PRESS

WHAT YOU NEED TO READ

For Ronan and Rachel

MERCIER PRESS
Cork
www. mercierpress.ie

Trade enquiries to CMD,
55A Spruce Avenue, Stillorgan Industrial Park,
Blackrock, County Dublin

© Pearse Lawlor, 2009

ISBN: 978 1 85635 612 1

10 9 8 7 6 5 4 3 2 1

A CIP record for this title is available from the British Library

 Mercier Press receives financial assistance from the Arts Council/
An Chomhairle Ealaíon

Printed and bound in the EU.

Contents

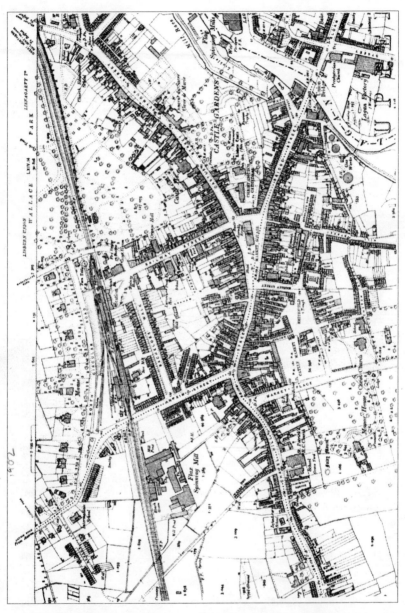

Map of Lisburn. *Reproduced from a 1902 Land and Property Services/ Ordnance Survey of Northern Ireland map*

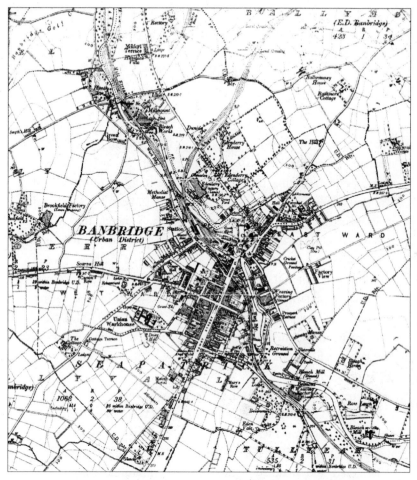

Map of Banbridge. *Reproduced from a 1902 Land and Property Services/ Ordnance Survey of Northern Ireland map*

PREFACE

This is an account of events in Ireland in 1920, and in particular the murders of two Royal Irish Constabulary officers. Many RIC officers were murdered during this period, but the murders of Divisional Commissioner Colonel Smyth and District Inspector Swanzy led to unprecedented reprisals against the Catholic population in the towns of Banbridge, Dromore and Lisburn. It traces the events which led to serious sectarian rioting and the burning of Catholic-owned property over a period of three months in 1920 and details, for the first time, the extent of the destruction and loss of life in these towns. The sectarian violence in Belfast between 1920 and 1922 has been well documented, but the scale of the violence in Belfast was such that events which took place in other towns, while mentioned, were never explored in detail.

To try to fully understand life in these northern towns at that time, it may be useful to recall what the world was like in 1920.

In 1920 the world was trying to come to terms with the aftermath of the Great War, the war to end all wars. Millions had been slaughtered and national economies were in ruins. The map of Europe changed, as did the lives of those who survived. The war was the result of political and economic rivalry in Europe and a growing sense of nationalism. People who had a common ethnic and linguistic background demanded the right to have independent states. When the war started in 1914, many young men from Ireland joined the British army, some to fight for the rights of the small nations and others, particularly from the north of Ireland, formed the 36th (Ulster) Division to fight for King and country.

In Ireland, the tide of nationalism which had ebbed and flowed over the previous centuries came crashing to the shore in 1916. Waves of nationalism had been rising steadily for over thirty years. The demand for a forum to represent Irish interests in Ireland, as opposed to England, had been vigorously pursued over the previous thirty-odd years by the Home Rule movement. Home Rule had been the main item on the political agenda for years and the issue was particularly divisive. The loyalist and mainly Protestant community in Ireland wished to retain their strong links and national identity with Britain. They knew that if Home Rule was introduced they would be a minority in a parliament filled with Irish Catholics, and where the Catholic Church would have a significant influence. They saw it as an attempt to establish a Roman Catholic ascendancy in Ireland and unionist politicians portrayed it as an attack on Protestantism. This dangerous mix of politics and religion, always a feature in Ireland, was played to maximum advantage by unionist politicians.

The loyalist population, mainly in the north-eastern counties of Ireland in the province of Ulster, was so totally opposed to the introduction of Home Rule that they were prepared to 'use all means which may be found necessary' to prevent the introduction of Home Rule. In 1912 almost half a million men and women, who could prove they were born in Ulster, signed the Ulster Covenant pledging to defeat by whatever means 'the conspiracy to set up a Home Rule parliament in Ireland'. The men who had signed the Covenant were invited to join the paramilitary Ulster Volunteer Force. In April of 1914, tons of arms and ammunition were smuggled into Ulster. The gun had been introduced to Irish politics and northern unionists were prepared to fight anyone, including the British, to retain their British links.

In the remainder of Ireland nationalism continued to surge and the Irish Volunteers, supporters of Home Rule, with guns and ammunition landed on a beach in County Wicklow and smuggled into Howth, provided opposition to the UVF. Civil war seemed inevitable.

In May 1914 loyalist fears were realised when the Home Rule Bill passed its third reading in the House of Commons and required only royal assent to become law. Negotiations nevertheless continued into July. Alarmed by the extent to which the opposing camps in Ireland were arming themselves, Prime Minister Asquith, influenced by Sir Edward Carson, decreed that the counties of Antrim, Down, Armagh and Londonderry would be excluded from the jurisdiction of Home Rule. The other counties of Ulster – Tyrone, Donegal, Cavan, Fermanagh and Monaghan – were deemed by Carson not to have sufficiently large Protestant populations to provide a safe majority.

By August 1914 the United Kingdom of Great Britain and Ireland was at war with Germany. Carson called on members of the UVF 'to answer his Majesty's call, as loyal subjects to the King'. Home Rule legislation was placed on hold. Civil war was avoided and men from the UVF and the Irish Volunteers set aside enmities and marched off to war.

Not all of the Irish Volunteers went to war. A small group, driven by the desire to restore Irish national identity and the Irish language, and to address appalling labour and social conditions in Ireland, decided to stage an insurrection. They were not content with the prospect of Home Rule sometime in the future, but wanted complete freedom from England. The insurrection took place on Easter Monday, 24 April 1916. Poorly organised because of conflicting orders, and mainly Dublin-based, it was doomed to fail. After five days of bloodshed and widespread destruction the rebels surrendered. It was not until the leaders of the Rising were executed, one by one, that the mood in Ireland changed. Initially the Rising had received little popular support, but the series of executions turned many against the British.

While 450 people lost their lives as a result of the Easter Rising, slaughter on a much larger scale was taking place in Europe. Several troops of young men who had joined the 36th (Ulster) Division left their trenches to march towards the German lines on 1 July 1916. The advancing soldiers were mown down by enemy machine-guns. That day and the following saw some 5,500 men of the Ulster Division killed or wounded. The Battle of the Somme would remain forever etched into the Ulster unionist psyche.

By 1918 the demand for manpower was increasing, as the killing on the battlefields of Europe continued. The British government decided to introduce conscription in Ireland. This was bitterly opposed by Irish nationalists, Sinn Féin and the Catholic church. In December 1916 Prime Minister Lloyd George had announced an amnesty for those who were rounded up and interned following the Easter Rising. Individuals like Michael Collins and Tomás MacCurtain had used their time in internment camps to plan for the future, and the release of these and other activists coincided with a rise in the popularity of Sinn Féin. Sinn Féin took the lead in opposing conscription and in the general election of December 1918 achieved a landslide victory. With renewed confidence they continued to press for Irish independence from Britain.

While discussions on Ireland's constitutional future were on-going, some members of the Irish Volunteers, later named the Irish Republican Army, frustrated at the slow rate of progress, took matters into their own hands. One of the earliest incidents was a raid on the Gortatlea RIC barracks in County Kerry on 10 April 1918 to obtain weapons. The Volunteers were outwitted by the RIC and one man was shot dead and another wounded. It was not the most auspicious start for the Volunteers in Kerry and was quietly allowed to slip from memory.[1] It was the murder in January 1919 of two policemen, during the theft of explosives at Soloheadbeg in

County Tipperary, which set in motion a chain of events that was to lead to a full-scale war for independence.

The Royal Irish Constabulary was the main target in the guerrilla war. Despite the introduction of extra military resources, supported by the Black and Tans and Auxiliaries in 1920, Britain achieved little success in an increasingly bloody war in Ireland. In the British parliament, Lloyd George introduced the Government of Ireland Bill on 22 December 1919, allowing for two parliaments in Ireland, one for six counties from the province of Ulster and one for the remaining twenty-six counties. This eventually received royal assent on 23 December 1920 and became the Government of Ireland Act.

The unionist population in the north, initially safe from the growing violence, became alarmed as attacks on police barracks moved further north. Now they were fearful not only for their lives but their whole way of life. The creeping influence of Sinn Féin hit home when in January 1920 the unionists lost control of Londonderry Corporation to Sinn Féin. Fears were further heightened when unionists lost a further ten Urban Councils to Sinn Féin. Many unionists felt that they had been abandoned by Britain and were unable to stem the growing tide of Sinn Féin influence.

Trouble had been brewing in Derry city following an outbreak of sectarian rioting caused by a traditional nationalist parade on the previous 15 August which had attempted to walk on Derry's walls, the preserve of loyalists for generations. The police had to call on the support of the army to quell the disturbances. The nationalist victory, a combination of Irish Parliamentary Party and Sinn Féin votes, at the municipal elections in January 1920 resulted in Alderman Hugh C. O'Doherty becoming the first Catholic mayor of the city since the siege of Derry in 1689. It had a dramatic impact on the Protestant and loyalist population, and Mayor O'Doherty did not exactly endear himself to the Protestant community when he said that he would not attend any function where there was likely to be a loyal toast. The tension that had been building up exploded in serious rioting on 16 April when it was claimed that soldiers of the Dorset Regiment had opened fire on a Catholic crowd in the city. The rioting soon escalated into gun battles between nationalists and the UVF. The UVF had been reorganised in the city to deal with the growing nationalist threat and took a leading part in the violence, including burning Catholic homes in retaliation for the eviction of Protestant families from Catholic areas of the city. The extent of the violence was such that 1,500 troops had to be called in to restore order. The troops sided with their ex-army comrades in the UVF. With the introduction of a curfew an uneasy peace was restored.

The death toll in this particular episode of sectarian violence was reckoned to be fifteen Catholics and four Protestants. Among the dead were Detective Sergeant Moroney from the RIC special branch and Howard McKay, the son of the governor of the Apprentice Boys. When news of McKay's death reached Belfast the shipyard workers telegraphed Carson, requesting that the UVF be mobilised to take revenge.[2] The violence in this city demonstrated how quickly sectarian attacks could flare out of control and result in deaths on both sides of the community. With the approach of July and heightened tension around the Twelfth of July celebrations, it was practically guaranteed that the violence would spread. When one of the many Protestants who left Derry for Belfast at this time spoke at a meeting of the ultra-loyalist Belfast Protestant Association at the Workman & Clark shipyard, explaining how Sinn Féin had taken control of Londonderry Corporation and providing his version of events, the die was cast in Belfast.

LISBURN

For the people of Lisburn 1920 was a time of unprecedented change and uncertainty. A quiet market town with a population of just over

12,000 it was a major centre of the linen industry in the north of Ireland. Factories such as William Barbour, Robert Stewart and the Island Spinning Company provided employment for 50 to 60 per cent of the working population of Lisburn. The demand for labour was such that many young men and women who would normally have worked on farms found secure employment in the many mills in Lisburn. Skilled young people, who worked in the linen mills elsewhere in the north of Ireland and had just married, were often persuaded to relocate to Lisburn by linen mill owners through the offer of a house. Many came from what were regarded as Catholic or nationalist areas and as children were born to these families the balance of the population gradually changed. Workers from both Catholic and Protestant backgrounds moved into houses in Lisburn and both communities were integrated, unlike Belfast, where co-religionists tended to live in the same areas. Mixed marriages were a common feature in Lisburn.

In other parts of northern Ireland it was often possible to tell a person's religion by their name – this was not the case in Lisburn. It was not unusual for two children from the same 'mixed marriage' family to attend schools of a different religious denomination. The war years were a boom time for the industry in Lisburn, as there was a constant demand from the army for material for knapsacks, webbing, etc. and from the air force for linen material for aeroplanes. Catholics and Protestants worked together in the mills to meet this demand.

Following the end of the war there was a severe economic recession that had a major impact on both Britain and Ireland. Among the industries to experience an economic downturn was the linen industry. Workers were made redundant and working hours were reduced to thirty hours a week. During the war years a fifty-five hour week was the norm, so the reduction in hours amounted to almost a 50 per cent cut in wages. Many ex-servicemen were unable to find employment upon discharge from the army. There was a certain bitterness among the mainly Protestant ex-servicemen, who had gone to fight for their country while many Catholics had remained at home, and these Catholics now enjoyed the luxury of being employed – though they were poorly paid. In Lisburn they were also faced with a growing Catholic population and an increasingly prosperous Catholic middle class of shopkeepers and publicans. In addition, a new and impressive church had been built on Chapel Hill twenty years previously to accommodate this growing Catholic population. The declining economic conditions resulted in rivalry between Protestants and Catholics for jobs. Religious discrimination in employment, which had been a fact of life on both sides of the religious divide for generations, but had largely ceased to be an issue during the war, now created growing tension between the two communities.

When politics were added to this, the situation became more volatile. Sir Edward Carson had visited Lisburn in February 1918 as part of a whistle-stop tour to cement opposition to Home Rule amongst the loyalist working class. The enthusiasm with which the loyalist population of Lisburn, under the leadership of the Orange Order, embraced the fight against Home Rule is perhaps best illustrated by an account of that visit.

All business in the town was suspended for the duration of the visit. Despite heavy and persistent rain a huge crowd gathered in Lisburn's Market Square. Orange brethren from Glenavy, Ballinderry, Derriaghy and Lisburn districts, wearing full regalia, assembled at the Orange Hall in Railway Street. Shortly after 2.30 p.m., headed by Lisburn Temperance Silver and Lisburn Conservative Fife and Drum bands, they proceeded to the outskirts of town to await the arrival of Sir Edward and his party. They waited in the pouring rain until 4.30 p.m., when the dignitaries finally arrived, and escorted them to a platform that had been erected in Market Square. The party included Lady Carson, Sir James Craig, Sir Robert and Lady Liddell and leading members of the Orange Order from Lisburn and surrounding areas. As part of his address he stated: '… that is the way we care to fight for our country because it means to us the liberties under which we live and that is why you and I and the people of Lisburn so highly value the country and the government in which and under which we exist – that we have shown in the past a persistent determination that no man shall lay a hand upon the privileges we possess'.

By 1920 events elsewhere in Ireland were causing the unionist population of Lisburn great concern. Home Rule was still promoted by unionist politicians such as Sir Edward Carson as the major issue, even though he had done a deal with the British prime minister to ensure that it would not apply to the counties in Ulster with a Protestant minority population. Opposition to Home Rule was not new to the people of Lisburn, nor was the message that it was linked to the Catholic church. As far back as August 1843 at a meeting of Lisburn Protestant Operatives Association Jonathan Richardson stated: 'I take the opportunity of assuring you that I think we ought to be thankful to God for having placed us in our present position and that it is our duty to endeavour to improve it rather than weaken it to the false cry of O'Connell and the popish priests who would not only dissolve our union with England and Scotland but would sever the ties of the Society by setting the poor against the rich and the tenant against the landlord that if one class suffer so might the other …' A poster from the same time read: 'Protestants, your peace, your prosperity and above all your duty to God demand the open avowal of your Principles against the traitorous attempt of Popish Ascendancy'. The message had changed little seventy-seven years later when Sir Edward Carson addressed an Orange demonstration at Finaghy on 12 July 1920.

By 1920 a combination of factors, including the growth of the Catholic population and a prosperous middle-class Catholic population, the success and vastly superior performance of Sinn Féin in the general election, the loss of unionist-controlled councils, declining economic conditions and the ever increasing threat of the IRA moving northwards, led to a feeling of insecurity and isolation among the Protestant unionist population, including that of Lisburn. During this time meetings had been taking place in Orange Halls to place the UVF on a war footing. Notices of these meetings were regularly advertised in the local unionist newspapers. The guns and ammunition that had been smuggled in and distributed in 1914 were still available in numerous arms caches and many 'trustworthy' UVF men had been allowed by their commanders to retain rifles at home. There was a clear sense of frustration. The unionist politicians who had so vociferously opposed Home Rule were telling their followers that Home Rule for northern Ireland, albeit on their own terms, should now be accepted. By July 1920, with anti-Catholic feeling encouraged by inflammatory speeches at Orange demonstrations, this sense of frustration, coupled with the association unionist politicians constantly made between the Roman Catholic religion and Sinn Féin, loyalism was like a powder keg. It would take little for the pent-up anger and frustration to explode in one of the worst outbreaks of sectarian violence in Ireland. All that was needed was an excuse.

1

Changing Times

As 1920 dawned there was more hope than expectation that the New Year would be better than the previous one.

It had been two years since the end of the Great War and the families who had lost loved ones hoped that they would never have to experience another war. In the cold and sober light of January it was clear that the war to end all wars had not, in fact, ended all wars. On the European mainland ethnic divisions had already led to further bloodshed. In Ireland the Anglo-Irish War, or the War of Independence, had begun the previous January and the ripples of the intermittent guerrilla-style attacks on crown forces gathered momentum and began to spread wider and wider. The Protestant loyalist population, particularly in the north-east of Ireland, saw the success of the IRA as a threat to plans for their own parliament and feared that they would be engulfed in a Catholic-dominated all-Ireland parliament. Unionist politicians did not trust the British government to deliver on its promise of a separate parliament for the north and made plans to resist by armed force, if necessary, any attempt by the British to force them into an Irish parliament. The Catholic population in the north-east equally feared that they could be isolated in a Protestant-dominated state and increasingly looked to the nationalist politicians and Sinn Féin to help prevent this happening. Sinn Féin however had a single, all-Ireland objective, the end of British rule in Ireland and the establishment of an Irish Republic. Its attention was focused on events in the south-west of

Ireland and because, in 1920, the prospect of a separate parliament in northern Ireland was not even on their agenda, the plight of the Catholic population in the north was not seen as a priority.

Initially the population in the northern part of Ireland seemed far removed from the events that were taking place in unfamiliar parts of Cork and Kerry, but as the weeks and months of 1920 ticked by, concern grew. The main and provincial newspapers in northern Ireland devoted more and more space to accounts of the attacks and deaths, or outrages as they were then known, that were taking place elsewhere in Ireland. Cork featured prominently in many of these reports, and it was two murders in the city of Cork, almost 300 miles away, that were to bring violence to Lisburn, Banbridge and other towns, and eventually communal warfare to the streets of Belfast.

2

The Murder of Tomás MacCurtain in Cork

Cork, a major city on the south coast of Ireland, saw itself as a rival to Dublin, the capital city. Like Dublin it had a strong manufacturing base and with its close proximity to the port of Queenstown (Cobh), a stopping-off point for transatlantic liners, it was an important trading centre. Henry Ford, whose parents came from Clonakilty in County Cork, had, in 1919, opened his first car assembly factory outside the United States in Cork, promoting the industrialisation of the city. When it came to politics and enthusiasm for the establishment of an Irish Republic, Cork was keen to show that it was on a par with its rival Dublin. It had, however, got off to a bad start.

During the Easter Rising in 1916 Irish Volunteers in Cork, under the leadership of the Irish Republican Brotherhood, were expected, like others throughout Ireland, to engage in an armed offensive against the British. Preparations had been made to form Volunteer companies throughout Cork and in Cork city Tomás MacCurtain, working as a clerk for coal importer Suttons, had been appointed as the commandant. Planning for the rising had been conducted in great secrecy and even the Volunteers' chief of staff, the moderate Eoin MacNeill, was not advised of the date of the rising.

In Cork a lot depended on the landing of German arms shipped from Lübeck. The plan was to land the arms at Fenit on Tralee Bay on Easter Sunday, and for the Volunteers in the province of Munster to march on the capital to support the Dublin Volunteers. A breakdown in communications about the exact arrival date and the fact that the ship did not have a radio resulted in a fiasco. The ship waited in Tralee Bay for instructions from shore and was even inspected by a British warship. The captain was successful in persuading a boarding party that it was a Norwegian ship with a cargo of timber. When no signals were received from shore the captain decided to abort the mission and to make a run for it. He was intercepted off the south-west coast of Ireland by the British warship *Bluebell* and ordered to proceed to Queenstown. The game was up and the captain scuttled his ship, the *Aud*, in Cork harbour. As the ammunition on board exploded and the arms sank to the bottom, the plans of the Munster Volunteers went with it.

When the insurrection started in Dublin on Easter Monday there was confusion and indecision in Cork. In Dublin Eoin MacNeill, on learning of the loss of the *Aud*, had issued an order countermanding previous instructions. Tomás MacCurtain was among those notified that the rising had been called off and as a result there was no decisive action on the day. The Volunteers who had been assembled to distribute the *Aud*'s arms were stood down and in Cork city there was a tense standoff between armed Volunteers and the British army. In a futile act of rebellion the Volunteers occupied their headquarters, the Volunteers Hall on Sheares Street. The leaders of the Volunteers in Cork spent that week restraining their men and conducting negotiations with Captain Wallace Dickie, representing the British military authorities, through Catholic Bishop Cohalan. At the end of the week they gave up their arms and were arrested without firing a single shot. Among those arrested was MacCurtain. The bishop successfully argued with the British that it had been agreed that there would be no arrests if the Volunteers' guns were handed over, and many of those arrested, including Tomás MacCurtain, were later released. On 11 May the British organised another series of arrests and MacCurtain was picked up at his home at 40 Thomas Davis

Street. He was brought to an internment camp at Frongoch in north Wales.

With the execution of the leaders of the rebellion in Dublin by the British, the mood in Cork changed, as it did throughout most of the country. With the leaders of the Cork Volunteers, including MacCurtain, released from Frongoch in time for Christmas 1916 (MacCurtain was not released until 24 December and did not arrive home until late on Christmas Day), they immediately set about reorganising. The humiliation felt by the leaders of the Cork Volunteers was such that they had to prove they were as capable as any in persuading the British to leave Ireland, and the time spent in the internment camp was used to plan an offensive against the British.

The Cork Brigade was re-established again under the leadership of Tomás MacCurtain and it was not long before he was re-arrested. On 26 February District Inspector Swanzy took him into custody along with his close friend and comrade Terence MacSwiney, and issued them with exclusion orders. MacCurtain was shipped over to Ledbury, in Herefordshire, England and ordered not to leave the area. However, by June 1917 he was once again free and back in Cork city. In October he was again arrested and this time was sent to Cork jail. He had defied a British government prohibition of Volunteers assembling or wearing uniforms by leading approximately 1,000 Volunteers on a march from Cork to Blarney to protest against the death of Thomas Ashe, who had taken part in the Easter Rising. Ashe had gone on hunger strike because he was not granted political status, and died after he was force-fed. Having spent a short time in Cork jail MacCurtain was released, but after only one day at home he was arrested again. When he refused to speak anything other than Irish when brought before the court, he was sentenced to six months in prison. By Christmas 1917, however, he was back on the streets.

The victory of Sinn Féin, a previously insignificant political party, at the general election of December 1918 boosted the confidence of young nationalist men and women and thousands joined the Volunteers (soon to be renamed the Irish Republican Army), or sympathised with their actions. From the humiliating failure in 1916 everything had changed. The IRA in Cork went on the offensive and soon killings on a previously unimaginable scale were a common occurrence. Cork was fast becoming the most violent county in Ireland and most of the early violence was directed at the Royal Irish Constabulary, which was seen by the Volunteers as the eyes and ears of the British government in Ireland.

By 1920 the Royal Irish Constabulary was a force under siege. In the outlying barracks policemen barricaded themselves in at night and very often made only token patrols during daylight hours. Under-resourced and with rapidly declining morale, a battalion of troops was sent to support them. They too came under attack. The barracks in Cork city had become fortresses, with steel shutters protecting the windows. Regular patrols were suspended at night and most of the force was employed in protecting the barracks from attack. Despite requests to the government for extra manpower, none was forthcoming and with limited police resources, in some cases only six constables to a barracks, the police were essentially powerless. The once prestigious policemen's status had been reduced to the point where they were isolated, ostracised by their fellow countrymen and even mocked in the street by children.

The government had in fact realised that the RIC was severely under-resourced and in September of the previous year Lieutenant-General Sir Frederick Shaw, the GOC in Ireland, had put forward a suggestion to quickly increase available manpower. He suggested that unemployed ex-servicemen in England and Scotland should be recruited to supplement the police force. On 7 October 1919, acting on advice from the Chief Secretary for Ireland Sir Ian Macpherson, the Cabinet approved the Shaw plan. Within a month press advertisements and posters called on ex-service men to take on a 'rough and dangerous task' in Ireland. The pay was 10 shillings per day. In the haste to recruit these men it was not possible to provide proper uniforms for them and a mixed uniform of dark green tunics and khaki trousers earned then the nickname the Black and Tans. In the summer of 1920 this group arrived in Ireland to support the RIC. With the arrival of the Black and Tans and later the Auxiliaries (ex-officers as opposed to ex-soldiers) with their mobile, well-armed and aggressive patrols, the situation began to change.

In the meantime senior commanders within the RIC were becoming increasing frustrated by what they saw as the government's failure to support them and the ever-increasing guerrilla tactics of the Volunteers' Cork brigade. The attitude of the police was perhaps best summed up in the report by the Chief Inspector of West Cork in June 1920:

> The police as a police force has ceased to exist. Irish Volunteers are tak-ing their place … the police are not consulted by the public who are afraid to be seen speaking to them.
>
> There is a feeling among the (West Cork) police which is becoming prevalent in places where murders of police have been committed that the only way to stop these murders is by way of reprisals or retaliation … It is becoming difficult to restrain men's passions aroused at the sight of their murdered comrades and when they have the means of executing vengeance it is likely that they will use them when driven to despera-tion.[1]

On 19 February 1920 the Volunteers, who were by then known as the Irish Republican Army, murdered Timothy Quinlisk outside the city. Quinlisk had been working for the British Secret Service and was attempting to track down Michael Collins, having been sent to Cork on a wild goose chase by an IRA contact in Dublin. He had made contact with the IRA in Cork and their suspicions that he might be a British agent were confirmed when Florence (Florrie) O'Donoghue, who was responsible for intelligence operations in the Cork IRA, held up a policeman on Cork's South Mall. O'Donoghue, along with Matt Ryan, a fellow intelligence officer, relieved him of a despatch case containing letters. One of the letters they particularly wanted to get their hands on confirmed their suspicions. Quinlisk was told he was to be shown a weapons cache, lured to a quiet area and shot. Florrie O'Donoghue later claimed that Timothy Quinlisk was Cork city's first fatality in the War of Independence.[2] He was to be the first of many.

On 10 March that year a municipal by-election took place and District Inspector McDonagh was on duty overseeing the guarding of the ballot boxes. While returning from this duty, along with Sergeant Ferris, he was shot and wounded. This was an opportunistic shooting: Florrie O'Donoghue and Tom Crofts, responsible for the Cork city active service unit, had been on patrol in Cork city centre, on the lookout for what were considered 'political' RIC men. Their objective, if the circumstances were right, was to shoot such officers. District Inspector McDonagh and Sergeant Ferris were high on that list and on the night of 10 March were walking unescorted along Southern Road when they came face to face with O'Donoghue and Crofts. Without any warning the IRA men drew their guns and opened fire on the unsuspecting police officers. O'Donoghue's gun jammed after a couple of shots and Crofts, firing several shots in quick succession, emptied his gun. Sergeant Ferris, from a position on the ground, returned fire, emptying his revolver at the assailants and grazing O'Donoghue. Miraculously, Ferris escaped uninjured and McDonagh was only wounded. An innocent passer-by was, however, seriously injured during the shooting. The IRA men disappeared into the night.

For many policemen in Cork city this was the last straw. That night policemen from throughout the city, armed with rifles, left their barracks and went on a rampage in search of Sinn Féiners. They vented their frustration by smashing windows, attacking houses and assaulting the occupants. DI Swanzy was on the streets with one of the police groups responsible for the widespread destruction. However, things began to get out of hand when a group of police officers decided they were going to shoot a number of Sinn Féin politicians as a reprisal for shooting District Inspector McDonagh.[3] Realising the implications of such action by the police, head constables and inspectors, including DI Swanzy, eventually succeeded in reining in their men, and the police were persuaded to return to their barracks. However, the frustration experienced by the constables was acknowledged by senior officers, and no disciplinary action was taken against any of the policemen, even though citizens had been assaulted and property damaged. From that night onwards the police in Cork city were a law unto themselves.

What the police found particularly galling was the fact that Tomás MacCurtain, the first officer commanding the Volunteers' Cork brigade, had also recently become lord mayor of Cork city. He had been elected following Sinn Féin's victory in the local elections of January 1920. MacCurtain, a married man with a young family, was top of the list for the police. While he commanded the IRA in Cork, his main interest was in longer-term strategy and politics. He did not always approve of the actions of his men, many of whom were in their teens and early twenties, and liable to undertake freelance operations without headquarter approval. He was considered by many to be too moderate. Despite close surveillance and numerous arrests, the police found it impossible to gather the necessary evidence to implicate him in the killings taking place in Cork.

Swanzy, who had been appointed District Inspector in Cork on

1 January 1916, was particularly active in tackling the threat posed by the Volunteers in Cork city. He had first-hand experience of the arrests of many Volunteers, including of course, Tomás MacCurtain. On 4 November 1918, police had raided the lodging house where Denis MacNeilus was living to search for illegal arms. MacNeilus was the quartermaster for Volunteers in the city and part of his duties was to repair arms. During the raid he shot and seriously wounded Head Constable Clarke. Police reinforcements were called for and arrived led by DI Swanzy. MacNeilus and another Volunteer who had come to his aid were arrested. Fearing that if the injured Head Constable died, MacNeilus would face a murder charge, the Volunteers decided to rescue him from Cork jail. They were successful, but while this helped raise the morale of the Volunteers, it also strengthened DI Swanzy's resolve to defeat the Volunteer movement.[4] He took a particular interest in MacCurtain, closely monitoring his every move to obtain the vital evidence which would lead to his arrest and conviction for murder. Swanzy was familiar with MacCurtain right from the start of his appointment as District Inspector, and had watched with concern the growth of the Cork Volunteers under MacCurtain's leadership. Swanzy was becoming frustrated because, despite the number of times MacCurtain had been arrested, it was all to no avail. Monitoring the speeches made by MacCurtain at public meetings, Swanzy once took him aside after a meeting and told him, 'It's not your meetings I mind, it is the youngsters.' It was a plea to keep the armed young hotheads in the Volunteers under control.

The plea fell on deaf ears. At 11 p.m. on 19 March 1920 forty-eight-year-old Joseph Murtagh, a constable with twenty-three years of service, was shot dead in Cork city by two IRA men, Christy Mac-Sweeney and J.J. O'Connell. Constable Murtagh was walking along Pope's Quay on his way back to his barracks. A widower with two grown-up children he lived in the Sunday's Well barracks, not far from where he was shot. He was off-duty and unarmed, and was returning from attending the funeral of a colleague, Constable Charles Healy. Healy had been killed a couple of days earlier, along with Constable James Rocke, as they left the chapel in Toomevara, outside Nenagh, following evening devotions on the feast day of Saint Patrick, the national saint.[5]

Constable Murtagh may have been seen by some as an inoffensive officer, keeping his head down until he got his pension, but to the IRA he had been a marked man for some time. He was regarded as a 'political' policeman who had taken a particularly aggressive stance against the local IRA. A month earlier Florrie O'Donoghue and Matt Ryan had been on the prowl in Cork city centre, specifically on the lookout for Constable Murtagh and Sergeant Ferris. They did not find Murtagh that night but spotted Ferris, along with two other policemen, as he left Tuckey Street barracks. The IRA men had their hands on their guns in their overcoat pockets, ready to shoot the officers. As they prepared to move out of the shadow of a doorway in Grand Parade, focused on their intended target, they failed to notice twelve to fourteen policemen coming up behind them. At the last minute they saw the approaching police and stood their ground, pretending to be having a conversation. The police group, which had probably come to escort Ferris, turned around, ignoring the two men in conversation, and made their way towards Union Quay barracks.

Constable Murtagh was not the only person making his way home that night. Also walking home was Tomás MacCurtain. He had spent the day at his office in the city hall taking care of civic duties, balancing his role in creating a new Ireland with directing a campaign to rid Ireland of the British. On his way home he called into his brigade headquarters, which was in Wallace's shop in St Augustine Street. The newsagent's was owned by sisters Sheila and Nora Wallace, who lived over the shop. The shop, open from eight in the morning until midnight, was used as the Volunteers' brigade headquarters. Meetings were held in the little kitchen at the back of the shop and it was used by Volunteers to drop and receive messages.[6]

Having discussed some brigade business he left with his colleague, Alderman Tadhg Barry, and his brother-in-law James Walsh and headed for his home above the family shop at 40 Thomas Davis Street. On the way he heard about the shooting of Constable Murtagh at Pope's Quay and immediately went to the Sinn Féin club on Watercourse Road. He advised all those present that, in view of the shooting on Pope's Quay, they should go to their homes. He was annoyed that the shooting had taken place, as it was yet another unauthorised killing. He spent some time on the telephone to the hospital to check on the constable's condition. When he heard that the constable had died he asked for his condolences to be passed to the Murtagh family. This may have been the lord mayor speaking, as opposed to the commander of Cork brigade. He would also have been aware that the killing put his own life in danger, as he had been warned that if the killing of RIC officers continued, this would be the case. He decided that an apology for the unauthorised killing should be issued and told those in the club, 'Who ever did it will pay the piper. We can't have men roaming around armed shooting police on their own.'[7] He left the club along with Peadar McCann and finally made his way home.

It was not only his wife, who was five months pregnant, and their five children – Siobhán, Síle, Máire, Tomás and baby Eilís – who lived in his home above the shop. His brother-in-law James and three sisters-in-law – Annie, Susie and Hannah – as well as two nieces, a nephew and his mother-in-law, who was an invalid, were also there. The extended family had moved from their home at Moorefield Terrace to avail of surplus accommodation on the upper floors of 40 Thomas Davis Street. They could also care for the invalid mother-in-law and the pregnant Elizabeth MacCurtain, who disliked being on her own while her husband was frequently absent in prison or away on Sinn Féin business. Tomás MacCurtain retired to bed at about midnight. The following day would be his thirty-sixth birthday.

In Union Quay barracks, Cork police headquarters, an important meeting had taken place on the afternoon of 19 March; plans were being made once again to arrest Tomás MacCurtain. Among those attending the meeting were Mr Clayton, recently promoted to Divisional Commander, County Inspector Maloney, who was new to Cork, and the locally-based and experienced DI Swanzy. County Inspector Maloney informed the meeting that he had received verbal instructions from the military to detail three men to meet a military lorry at 2 a.m. on 20 March at the home of Tomás MacCurtain who was to be arrested. He delegated this task to DI Swanzy, who had responsibility for Cork (north). Later in the afternoon, at about 5 p.m., DI Swanzy, at the four-storey King Street barracks, was presented with a typewritten document ordering the arrest of MacCurtain and confirming the arrest time as 2 a.m. He detailed Head Constable Cahill from King Street barracks to organise the men to accompany the military and at 11 p.m., the time at which one of his colleagues, Constable Joe Murtagh, was shot dead at Pope's Quay, Cahill assigned the task to Sergeant Beatty. Beatty suggested that the military call at King Street barracks and proceed from there to Tomás MacCurtain's home.

At about 2.15 a.m. Lieutenant D.F. Cooke, with a lorry and twenty men, arrived at King Street barracks to be advised which houses were to be raided that night. Sergeant Beatty, along with Constables Sullivan, Murphy and Walsh, left with the military party for 40 Thomas Davis Street. When they pulled up outside MacCurtain's shop all was not as they had expected – silent and with everyone fast asleep. The front door was open, there were lights on in the house and people in a distressed state were milling about in the street. It was obvious that something had happened. Lieutenant Cooke was informed that Tomás MacCurtain had been shot dead about an hour earlier.

It was at about 1.30 a.m. that Mrs MacCurtain heard a knocking at the front door. This was not unusual, as it was a regular occurrence for the house to be raided by the military. She went to the front window, looked into the street to see what was happening and called out to ask who was there. The knocking intensified and was followed by the sound of the door being kicked. She was told to come down. Tomás woke from his sleep, pulled on his trousers and said he would go down, but his wife lit a candle and, dressed in her nightdress, made her way down the narrow stairway to the front door. She appealed to those outside to wait until she had time to dress, but was told to open the door immediately or it would be broken down. Reluctantly she opened the door and two men with darkened faces and carrying revolvers rushed in and demanded to know where MacCurtain was. A further six men, armed with rifles, proceeded to force their way into MacCurtain's home.[8] Mrs MacCurtain was restrained at the front door while the armed men with darkened faces bounded up the stairs.

Susie Walsh, Tomás' sister-in-law, called to her brother and was first to jump out of bed, alarmed by the noise downstairs. She pulled on her red overcoat and from her bedroom door saw two men at the door of Tomás' bedroom, one with a light-coloured coat and a cap, with his face blackened, shouting for him to come out. She pleaded, to no avail, to be allowed to take the ten-month-old baby, who was crying, out of the room. She was told to 'get back out of that' and took refuge in the bathroom.

James Walsh, Tomás' brother-in-law, also awoken by the noise, was making his way down from the top landing by the light of a candle when he saw two tall men facing Tomás, who by this time had come to the door of his bedroom. Two shots were fired in quick succession, followed by a third. The assassins then battered his head with rifle butts before making their escape. James immediately extinguished the candle and dropped to the floor as he listened to the men run down the stairs. He went to a front window and as he called for help shots were fired at the window. The assassins, it was reported, escaped in a waiting motor car.[9]

Tomás had been shot point-blank in the chest and was bleeding heavily. Annie, the other sister-in-law, tried to comfort the dying man. With the men gone from the house, Mrs MacCurtain ran to get her husband a drink of water and telephoned the telephone exchange to get them to contact a doctor and a priest. The local priest, Fr Butts from North Cathedral, arrived and administered the last sacraments. Doctor O'Connor rushed to the scene and climbed the stairs to where Elizabeth had been cradling her dying husband. There was nothing the doctor could do and he pronounced Tomás dead. It was then that the police and army arrived.

On hearing that a shooting had taken place, the police refused to enter the building. The military personnel, despite being told that the man they had come to arrest had been murdered a short time previously, moved in to conduct a search of the premises. MacCurtain's body had by this time been laid out on his bed, but that did not prevent the military from searching under the mattress. (Fionnuala MacCurtain in her book *Remember it's for Ireland* states that her grandfather's body was tossed to the floor as the soldiers searched under the mattress). Following a thorough search of the house, during which nothing was found, the soldiers left. They had missed Tomás' personal revolver, which had been hidden under the mattress of baby Eilís' pram in the MacCurtains' bedroom.

It was later claimed at the coroner's inquest that Thomas Davis Street, close to Blackpool police barracks, had been blocked off by a large number of masked and disguised men armed with rifles while the murder was taking place. The police 'Report of Outrage', completed after the murder, records that Blackpool barracks was only 100 yards from the murder scene. One section of the report, question seven, asks: 'When (stating the hour) did the District Inspector visit the scene?' The form was completed stating: 'Not allowed to visit scene by friends of the deceased who were there in hundreds.'[10] As soon as word spread about the murder of the lord mayor, a number of Volunteers arrived to lay out the body in full uniform, and they stood through the night, as a guard of honour, beside their comrade. By early morning hundreds thronged the street outside the MacCurtain home.

The funeral of Tomás MacCurtain took place on Monday 22 March. In a scene unlike any previously witnessed in Cork, the entire city came to a standstill, with every shop and factory closed. The cortège left Cork cathedral at 1 p.m. and the pregnant Elizabeth and her children were joined by thousands who stood in silence as the horse-drawn hearse, the top of which was completely covered in wreaths, made its way along the funeral route to the cemetery. Elizabeth was to experience further sorrow when the twins she was carrying were stillborn four months later.

T.P. O'Connor, MP, later raised the matter of the murder in the House of Commons and suggested that the purpose of the raid by the military after the murder was to destroy evidence. The police made no attempt to investigate the crime and placed the blame on rogue elements within the IRA who felt that MacCurtain was too soft in the fight against the British. It was not to be the last such killing. Operating under the cover name of the Anti-Sinn Féin Society, a death squad had emerged within the RIC in Cork. Threatening letters issued by the Anti-Sinn Féin Society to give the impression that it was a widespread secret society, were usually followed by killings which received the tacit support of the local District Inspector.[11]

An inquest into the murder of Tomás MacCurtain, in which ninety-seven witnesses were examined, sixty-four of them being police, thirty-one civilians and two military, was conducted by coroner James J. McCabe. The inquest was opened on 20 March and concluded on 17 April with the following unanimous verdict:

> We find that the late Alderman MacCurtain, Lord Mayor of Cork, died from shock and haemorrhage caused by bullet wounds, and that he was wilfully murdered under circumstances of the most callous brutality, and that the murder was organised and carried out by the Royal Irish Constabulary, officially directed by the British Government, and we return a verdict of wilful murder against David Lloyd George, Prime Minister of England; Lord French, Lord Lieutenant of Ireland; Ian McPherson, late Chief Secretary of Ireland; Acting Inspector General Smith, of the Royal Irish Constabulary; Divisional Inspector Clayton of the Royal Irish Constabulary; DI Swanzy and some unknown members of the Royal Irish Constabulary. We strongly condemn the system at present in vogue of carrying out raids at unreasonable hours. We tender to Mrs MacCurtain and family our sincerest sympathy. We extend to the citizens of Cork our sympathy in the loss they have sustained by the death of one so eminently capable of directing their civic administration.

In a letter written by Terence MacSwiney dated 24 April 1920, to Lady Fitzgerald Arnott, thanking her for a £10 subscription to the MacCurtain Memorial Fund, he commented on events during the night Tomás MacCurtain was murdered. The murder party, accompanied by policemen in uniform, had been seen in King Street, on St Patrick's Hill and in the Blackpool area. A nurse called Daunt had seen the group from the private hospital where she worked. Two uniformed policemen redirected a passer-by named McCarthy away from the MacCurtain home at the time when the murder was about to take place. A lamplighter named Desmond had, at twenty minutes to two, witnessed a body of men carrying rifles march quickly in single file towards King Street barracks. Following a light knock on the door they were admitted to the barracks. MacSwiney went on to quote a statement made at the inquest by the crown solicitor that this was a murder in which between forty and fifty men were engaged.[12]

When word reached Michael Collins that his comrade Tomás MacCurtain had been assassinated and that named individuals in the Royal Irish Constabulary were being held responsible, he promised revenge. Since he had been released from internment following his part in the Easter Rising in 1916, Collins had been elected to the executive committee of Sinn Féin and was responsible for the guerrilla tactics of the IRA in attacking both the RIC and the British army. He believed in an eye for an eye. By 1920 he had been appointed as Minister for Finance in the Dáil government and was also Director of Intelligence of the IRA. Tomás MacCurtain was a fellow Corkman and they had both been interned in the Frongoch internment camp in Wales. There had been a close bond between Collins and MacCurtain. At the end of 1919 Collins and MacCurtain were part of the group that planned one of the many unsuccessful attempts to ambush and kill Lord French, the Lord Lieutenant of Ireland.[13] Collins set about using the formidable resources available to him to avenge the killing of his friend. The key resource available to Collins was the extensive intelligence network he had created which even penetrated Dublin Castle, the seat of British rule in Ireland. Instructions went out to track down those responsible for the murder of Tomás MacCurtain.

3

Swanzy leaves Cork

Because DI Swanzy had been specifically named at the inquest as having been involved in the murder of the lord mayor it was decided by the authorities that, for his own safety, he should be transferred from Cork. This decision was made even more urgent following the murder on 11 May of Sergeant Denis Garvey, who had figured prominently at the inquest of Tomás MacCurtain. The IRA believed that Garvey and Constable Harrington were responsible for the murder and that they had fired the shots that killed MacCurtain. Sergeant Garvey, along with Constables Harrington and Doyle, had left the Lower Glanmire Road barracks and had boarded a tram car. As they took their seats a number of men who were already on the tram drew revolvers and shot the three police officers. The assassination team was led by Patrick 'Pa' Murray who, as Commander of the Cork city active service unit, was well versed in such attacks. Only Constable Doyle survived the attack.[1]

It was now essential that a new posting be found for DI Swanzy, well away from the IRA's Cork brigade. On 15 May he was transferred. He disappeared suddenly, leaving the city secretly by train, the warrant for his ticket issued under an assumed name. However, little happened in Cork that did not come to the attention of the IRA. Florrie O'Donoghue had created a situation in which every IRA volunteer was tasked with gathering intelligence information, and this extended to civilian sympathisers. Staff at railway stations and hotels were an important asset and IRA commander Connie Neenan later recalled, 'We had staff in every hotel. You could not enter Cork at that time without us knowing all the details about you.'[2] It seemed to also be true that you could not leave Cork without the IRA knowing about you. Seán Healy, a railway man, was curious about the well-dressed man who seemed to be leaving in a hurry without being burdened by luggage – he had asked for his luggage to be forwarded separately. Healy later examined the luggage and Swanzy's initials, O.R.S., were discovered on a box, confirming the identity of the real owner. The destination for the luggage was Lisburn.[3]

On 15 June that year he was appointed District Inspector in Lisburn, a predominately loyalist town in the north of Ireland. There had been a vacant District Inspector's post in Lisburn following the promotion earlier in the year of Vere R.T. Gregory. He had served in Lisburn as District Inspector since 1910 and now had risen to the rank of County Inspector.[4] Swanzy, a single man, moved in with his mother and sister Irene in their home at 31 Railway Street, just opposite the Orange Hall. It was close to the centre of Lisburn town and conveniently located, as it was a short stroll to the police barracks. Before taking up his duties he took a holiday on the Isle of Man, a world away from the tensions and intrigue in Cork – but even there he looked over his shoulder.

Lisburn was an area that had been spared the type of violence and murder that had become commonplace in Cork. The police there could carry out the normal police duties dealing with petty theft, citizens who had had too much to drink and people who did not have lights on their bicycles. The local policemen dreaded a posting to counties Cork or Kerry, and one sergeant had a mental breakdown when he received notification of a transfer to County Kerry. For DI Swanzy, coming north was a welcome relief.

However events were taking place in County Kerry which would bring not republican but loyalist violence to the streets of Belfast, Banbridge, Dromore, Lisburn and other towns.

4

The Listowel Mutiny

The rate of attrition within the Royal Irish Constabulary in the south-west of Ireland was increasing day by day and it was obvious that the force could not keep up with the hit-and-run tactics adopted by the IRA. The British government decided that there would have to be a radical change of policy in order to gain the upper hand in this undeclared war. In future the military would have primacy in the battle against the IRA; it would no longer simply provide support to the RIC, but would take a more proactive role in tackling the enemy. Roles were to be reversed.

This change of policy came to the public's attention in Listowel, County Kerry, through an incident that was to have widespread repercussions in both England and Ireland. Listowel was a relatively quiet market town where the police were able to conduct unarmed patrols during the day. At night they took the precaution of carrying carbines or revolvers, but were spared the attacks that were occurring elsewhere. The most pressing duty for the police in Listowel was to protect Michael O'Brien, a land steward employed by Ella Frances Browne, heiress of the Gunn Estate of Rattoo, who was under threat because of the ongoing agrarian dispute. The monthly Chief Inspector's reports at that time concentrated as much on the agrarian disputes as the disturbances and attacks taking place in their districts.

Early in 1920 English and Scottish ex-servicemen began to filter into the RIC as 'policemen', attracted by a payment of 10 shillings per day. Two were posted to Listowel barracks, although neither had received any police training. This was part of the advance guard for the previously mentioned Black and Tans. Changes were not only taking place on the ground; senior officers in the RIC were being replaced with younger, more aggressive officers. Following MacCurtain's murder in March that year, the attitude of the police and military in counties Cork, Limerick and Tipperary changed. There was a steady drift from maintaining law and order to reprisals, destruction and terror. The RIC men located in Listowel barracks, the district headquarters, observed with some concern that the uneasy peace they had been experiencing was about to come to an end.

Change came swiftly and unexpectedly. On 16 June 1920, following a telephone call from Poer O'Shee, RIC County Inspector in Tralee, to District Inspector Flanagan in Listowel, a constable was detailed to collect an urgent despatch being sent by rail to Listowel railway station. The despatch contained instructions to transfer fourteen officers to other barracks with immediate effect. They had to be out of the barracks by noon the following day. The military were to take control of the barracks and only one constable and two sergeants were to remain to support the military, who would be under the command of Captain Chadwick.

The police in Listowel were informed that, as part of the new policy, they were to hand over their barracks to the military. They were told that they would have to accept transfers to other barracks in the district where they would provide intelligence for the military and act as scouts for military patrols. The police constables, on hearing this unexpected news, adjourned to the dining-room in the barracks and held a meeting to discuss being downgraded and the change of command. Unhappy with the prospect of being transferred and having to report to military commanders who had no knowledge of police work, they decided to challenge the order. They decided to 'hold the barracks'. Constable Jeremiah Mee was selected as the spokesman for the constables. After the meeting, when they had discussed the options open to them, he telephoned the County Inspector in Tralee who had issued the instructions and informed him that he and the men in the barracks were not prepared to accept the order. The County Inspector listened in silence and then put the phone down. Mee and his colleagues realised they were in trouble. A short time later the telephone in the District Inspector's office rang. It was the County Inspector, telling him to have all the men in the barracks on parade at 10 a.m. the following day.

The following day, 17 June, at 10 a.m. sharp, County Inspector Poer O'Shee arrived at Listowel barracks to enforce the order. Facing the assembled men he asked if they were refusing to obey an order of the Divisional Commissioner. He told them that if the answer was yes, they should resign. The men replied that they were not prepared to accept the changes that were to be imposed on them and fourteen threatened to resign. Faced with this embarrassing and serious situation, O'Shee left the barracks in a rage, advising them that, 'You will hear more about this'.

On Saturday 19 June the constables in Listowel barracks were once again ordered to be on parade at 10 a.m. As they stood in silence in the dayroom, each man contemplating the seriousness of the action they had embarked on, they heard the familiar sound of a Crossley tender arriving outside the barracks. The dayroom faced the street and they saw fifteen fully armed and helmeted policemen and three high-ranking officers in full dress uniforms alight from the vehicle. Another Crossley, packed with fully armed soldiers, pulled in behind them. A third Crossley containing more armed police then drew up. The occupants climbed out of the tenders, some having travelled across country from Dublin Castle, and gladly stretched their legs. Cigarettes and cigars were lit, and the men stood chatting in small groups on the lawn and pathway outside the barracks as they appeared to wait for something before entering the barracks. The men inside watched with increasing alarm.

A short time later another Crossley containing more soldiers came to a halt outside the barracks. A tall, imposing officer, his uniform resplendent with medals glinting in the bright morning sunshine, dismounted from the cab. This was the man they all had been waiting for. His name was Colonel Smyth.[1]

Colonel Gerald Brice Ferguson Smyth

Colonel Gerald Brice Smyth had been born on 7 September 1885 at Phoenix Lodge, Dalousie, in the Punjab region of India, the first son of George Smyth from Milltown, Banbridge, who was then the British High Commissioner in the Punjab region, and Helen Ferguson, daughter of Thomas Ferguson of Edenderry House, Banbridge. Both the Smyth and Ferguson families were linen barons in Banbridge. He was educated in England at Shrewsbury School and later had private tuition by William Thompson Kirkpatrick, the former head of Lurgan College, who incidentally later tutored the author C.S. Lewis.[2] He gained a first place entrance to the Royal Military Academy, Woolwich on 2 September 1903 and joined the Royal Engineers on 29 July 1905.[3]

A well-educated individual who excelled at mathematics and Spanish, he had passed up an academic career as Chair of Mathematics at Chatham College to serve his country in 1914 at the outbreak of the war. He saw action in the Aisne area of France and it was there that, in attempting to rescue a wounded colleague during heavy shellfire, he was severely injured by shrapnel. His injuries resulted in his left arm being amputated below the elbow in a field ambulance. He would later be affectionately known as 'DSO the one arm'. After a period in hospital he returned to the front as second in command of the 90th Field Company of the 9th Division.

He was later injured when a bomb exploded prematurely and he also survived the Battle of the Somme, despite being shot in the neck. In fact he was wounded some six times during the war. Each time as he recovered from his injuries, he requested to be reinstated for active service. Awarded the DSO with Bar, Croix de Guerre, French and Belgian, and mentioned eight times in despatches, there could be no doubt about his credentials as a battle-hardened soldier and a leader. In Ireland, however, he was dealing with a different kind of enemy in a different type of war.

Following the war he attended the army staff college and was regarded as an officer with great potential. He was a man who was prepared to consider revolutionary military methods, and at the college he was known as 'Trotsky' – he may have subscribed to Trotsky's view that nothing should get in the way of military success.[4] Trotsky wrote in his autobiography: 'An army cannot be built without reprisals. Masses of men cannot be led to death unless the army command has the death penalty in its arsenal.' While these measures applied mainly to soldiers refusing orders, it also had wider implications.

After his time in the staff college he was posted to Ireland to command the 12th Field Company, Royal Engineers as brevet lieutenant-colonel. The 12th Field Company had transferred to Limerick on 6 June 1919 and would remain there until 28 February 1922. One advantage of this posting was that it enabled him to travel more frequently to the family home in Banbridge. It was from there that, on 31 December 1919, having spent Christmas with his widowed mother, he left to take up the new post in Limerick. There had been heavy snowfall overnight and snow was still on the ground when he caught the 3 p.m. train from Banbridge. With a change of trains at Scarva he arrived in Dublin at 6 p.m. He was accompanied on this leg of the journey by his cousin, Howard Ferguson Murland, a lieutenant in the Indian army.[5] Based in Limerick, he was looking forward to spending his spare time engaged in country pursuits, particularly hunting. That, however, was not to be. Soon after his arrival he was offered a policing role. He had served with Major General Tudor in the 9th Scottish Division and it was Tudor who appointed him, or had been instructed to appoint him, as one of the new RIC Divisional Commissioners in Ireland. Major General Hugh Tudor had been appointed by the government as police adviser in Ireland, on the recommendation of his close friend Winston Churchill. He took up his post in Dublin Castle in May 1920 and set about implementing Churchill's policy to sweep away the old RIC command structure.

Colonel Smyth would officially take up the post of Divisional Commissioner for the province of Munster on 3 June 1920. While he readily accepted this challenging post, his mother was less enthusiastic about it. She confided to her friend, Miss Alice Henderson who lived at 6 Cambridge Square in London, that her hopes for peace of mind had gone and the war had begun for her again.

Colonel Smyth took advantage of the good railway network in Ireland to return home. In March he was back in Banbridge and on 9 March 1920 was staying at Ardnabannon, the home of another cousin, James Warren Murland.[6] The Murland family, like the Smyth and Ferguson families, was engaged in the linen industry and had a flax-spinning, linen-manufacturing and bleaching factory at Annsborough, near Castlewellan. The Smyths and the Murlands were particularly close. Colonel Smyth's aunt, Sarah Ferguson, had married Clotworthy Warren Murland. It was to Ardnabannon that Colonel Smyth's brother Osbert had gone to recuperate having been wounded by shrapnel on 21 December 1915. That injury resulted in him being unable to fully flex his left arm.

The Murlands, like the other linen barons in the north of Ireland, were staunchly loyalist. They were utterly opposed to Home Rule, not only from a personal point of view, but also from a business perspective. Murland traded internationally and before the outbreak of the Great War had offices in London, Berlin, Paris and New York as well as Belfast and Glasgow. It was essential for him to retain the link with Britain, and the family would have looked disdainfully at the agriculture-based economy in the south of Ireland. The Murland brothers became heavily involved in the establishment of the UVF in south County Down in order to maintain this link by force, if necessary. In 1913 Charlie (Charles Henry) Murland was the secretary responsible for organising the UVF in County Down. He later commanded the Castlewellan Company. At a Volunteer's parade on 24 May 1914 Warren Murland, flanked by armed UVF men, was photographed carrying the King's colours. The colours, along with those of the South Down UVF, were later placed on a Lambeg drum, reinforcing the link with the Orange Order, and were blessed by the Dean of Down.

Arms and ammunition had been imported on a large scale the previous month on the night of 24 April and had been dispersed to prepared arms dumps throughout Ulster, including the Murland factory. Howard Ferguson Murland recorded in his diary on 25 June 1914 how he and Warren had driven to Murlough 'with a cargo of ammunition' before he went out on the sand hills to watch the North Irish Horse Regiment on manoeuvres.

Colonel Smyth would have been aware of the Murland family's involvement with the UVF when he made that visit to Ardnabannon House in March 1920. This link with family members, who were leaders of the UVF, would not have been seen as an impediment to General Tudor's plan to replace the RIC Divisional Commissioners with young, handpicked former army officers, such as Colonel Smyth, capable of implementing a new government-approved strategy to bring to an end the war being waged by the IRA. The new policy came to light a matter of days after Tudor's appointment. The Divisional Commander in Limerick recorded: 'I have been told the new policy and plan and I am satisfied, though I doubt its ultimate success in the main particular – the stamping out of terrorism by secret murder. I still am of the opinion that instant retaliation is the only course for this.'[7] Proof of the government's policy would come on 8 July 1920 when Winston Churchill, as Secretary of State for War, stood up in the House of Commons to seek approval for a contribution of £53,000 towards the cost of the Department of the Secretary of State for India. It was known that this debate would widen to deal with events in Amritsar the previous year and the public gallery was packed.

At that time there had been a growing campaign to bring the rule of the British Raj in India to an end and on 10–12 April 1919 there were riots in a number of Indian cities including Amritsar. The governor of the Punjab, Sir Michael O'Dwyer, the son of a Catholic Irish landowner from Tipperary, believed that these riots were coordinated and were the beginning of a full-scale insurrection to overthrow the Raj. The riots in Amritsar, in protest at the arrest of two leading nationalists, soon turned to an attack on Europeans and their property. O'Dwyer called on Brigadier-General Reginald (Rex) Dyer to help restore order.

He arrived on the evening of 11 April to find that the European population had taken refuge in a fort and that the city was in the hands of the rioters. With over 1,100 troops under his command, one-third of whom were British, he led a show of force through the city the following morning. Rumours of a possible mutiny by Indian troops and fear that a mass demonstration planned for the afternoon of 13 April was the prelude to a major insurrection, convinced Dyer that the only way to resolve the situation was to 'strike terror into the whole of the Punjab'.

When an estimated 15–20,000 people gathered in an enclosed area known as Jallianwala Bagh Dyer deployed his men to face the crowd and, without warning, in a planned operation, ordered them to open fire on the crowd. The soldiers continued firing for ten minutes, in fact until they were almost out of ammunition. During those ten minutes over 1,650 rounds of .303 ammunition had been fired and 379 lay in the dust dead or dying with 1,500 wounded, many trampled underfoot as thousands fled in panic.[8] When the noise of the gunfire ceased Dyer and his men surveyed the bodies of the dead and dying, turned their backs to them, and left. Dyer later stated that he would like to have killed more and regretted not being able to get two armoured cars with machine guns into position because of the narrow entrances.

Later as a punishment for attacking, and leaving for dead, an English missionary doctor, Marcia Sherwood, Dyer forced the residents living in the area where she had been attacked to crawl along the alley on their stomachs. They had to make their way through a drainage canal filled with animal and human excrement and were supervised by soldiers with fixed bayonets. This was despite the fact that Miss Sherwood had been rescued by some locals who lived in the narrow alley and had taken her to the safety of the fort. The 'Crawling Order' was imposed for two weeks until it came to the attention of the viceroy Lord Chelmsford who immediately ordered that it should cease. Shopkeepers were taken from shops and flogged if they did not sell goods to British soldiers at reduced prices.[9]

A news blackout was imposed after the massacre to prevent the British public learning of the mass murder in Amritsar, but eventually Indian sources brought it to public attention. When Dyer returned to England in May of that year he was ordered to resign his command. The British public, fed stories by the ultra-Conservative press of how he had saved the Raj, contributed to a fund to reward Dyer for 'having saved India'. A figure of over £26,000 eased his enforced retirement. (Dyer was later exonerated by the House of Lords. O'Dwyer was shot dead in Caxton Hall in London on 13 March 1940 by a Sikh nationalist in revenge for the Amritsar massacre).

The debate in the House of Commons on the 8 July did widen to include Amritsar and comments regarding Dyer's actions in Amritsar were heated with a number of members supporting Dyer. Among those who supported him was Sir Edward Carson who argued that Dyer had nipped a revolution, part of a global plot, in the bud. 'It is all one conspiracy, it is engineered in the same way, it has the same object – to destroy our sea-power and drive us out of Asia.'[10] (He saw it as a communist plot against the British Empire linked to anti-British movements in India, Egypt, Iraq and of course in Ireland). He went on to say, 'It must be remembered that when a rebellion has been started against the government it is tantamount to a declaration of war, and war cannot be conducted in accordance with the standards of humanity to which we are accustomed in peace.'

Churchill denounced to the House what he called the 'frightfulness' in the Punjab and approved of Dyer's resignation. In private however it was claimed that Churchill considered that Dyer had been right to 'shoot hard' and right to remove his men without taking care of the wounded. He did however reveal his true feelings when he said, without any evidence, that the demonstrators were armed: 'Men who take up arms against the state must expect at any moment to be fired on. Men who take up arms unlawfully cannot expect that troops will wait until they are quite ready to begin the conflict.' He was interrupted by Mr McDonald who asked, 'What about Ireland?' Churchill continued, 'I agree and it is in regard to Ireland that I am specially making this remark.'[11]

The policy had already been implemented a couple of months earlier with the murder of Tomás MacCurtain in Cork, and would continue with the introduction by General Tudor, as police advisor, of the Black and Tans and the Auxiliaries – another Churchill initiative. Terror and not so secret state murder would follow.

The Listowel Mutiny (continued)

With the arrival of Colonel Smyth at Listowel barracks, cigarettes were extinguished and uniforms straightened. The waiting group comprised the Inspector General, General Tudor, the Commissioner of Police from Dublin Castle, in full dress uniform with medals and his white ostrich feather headdress, Major Letham, the County Inspector, George B. Heard, Captain Chadwick and Assistant County Inspector Dobbyn. Protected by a military escort they marched up the pathway to the arched doorway of the substantial three-storey Listowel barracks with the intention of laying down the law.

Within days of being appointed to a policing role, Colonel Smyth had produced a number of written orders to the men in his command. In an order dated 10 June he instructed that the number of police stationed at the new combined military/police barracks would be reduced to a minimum, with only those with good local knowledge retained. An indication of the harder line that he proposed to take related to barracks that were abandoned by the RIC, who then had to join the military in garrisons. As it was normal for the IRA to burn such barracks to prevent the RIC returning, his order was for the RIC to select the house of a leading local Sinn Féiner and to pass the details on to him. He personally would issue an order to requisition that house if the barracks was attacked. The occupier was to be warned that if the barracks was burned, his house would be seized and he would be given twenty-four hours before being evicted and the house emptied. That house would become the *de facto* barracks and the procedure would be repeated if that house came under attack.[12] These instructions however had not been relayed to Listowel barracks by the time Colonel Smyth arrived and the RIC men in the barracks had no knowledge of these instructions or indeed any idea of the identity of this tall, one-armed officer.

Despite the presence of the senior ranking officer, General Tudor, Colonel Smyth took the lead in addressing the Listowel RIC men. Flanked by his colleagues lined up in front of the fireplace, he wasted no time in impressing his authority and credibility upon the group of constables he was facing. He started by informing the men standing to attention that he had been appointed by the prime minister of England and that he reported directly to the prime minister. He explained the government's policy for dealing with the exceptional circumstances the country was facing. The government's stated policy was that 'it is determined to suppress violence and punish perpetrators of it by every means in their power. Sinn Féin fanatics are to be met with arms. Soldiers will become, for the time, policemen aiding in every way the Royal Irish Constabulary, a brave body of men who have lately been too few in number to deal with the organised terrorism in their midst.'[13] As part of his address, reading from an order that he had prepared and signed a few days earlier, on 17 June, he stated:

I wish to make the present situation clear to all ranks. A policeman is perfectly justified in shooting any person seen with arms who does not immediately throw up his hands when ordered. A policeman is perfectly justified in shooting any man who he has good reason to believe is carrying arms and who does not immediately throw up his arms when ordered. Every proper precaution will be taken at police inquests that no information will be given to Sinn Féin as to the identity of any individual or the movements of the police.

He also went on to say: 'I wish to make it perfectly clear to all ranks that I will not tolerate reprisals. They will bring discredit on the police and I will deal severely with any officer or man concerned in them.'

This last statement is somewhat at odds with his previous instructions regarding vacated barracks and the plan to evict local Sinn Féin home-owners.

He informed them that from that point onwards the military would take the offensive and beat the republicans at their own game. Martial law would be introduced with immediate effect and on 21 June the RIC and military would be amalgamated. Together, the police and military would adopt a ruthless approach to quell the rebellion in the country. He said that he had been promised as many troops from England as he required and added that thousands were coming daily.

He went on to explain an innovative and proactive policy that would be used years later by the British Army's Special Air Services (SAS). His policy was that police and military would patrol the country at least five nights a week. They were not to confine themselves to the main roads but to move across the country and to lie in ambush. When civilians approached, the order 'Hands up!' would be given. If this order was not immediately obeyed they were to shoot and shoot with effect. If persons approaching had their hands in their pockets or were suspicious-looking, the order was to shoot them down. He admitted that mistakes might occasionally be made and innocent people shot, but that could not be helped. He went on to say that if innocent people were killed he would see to it that no policeman would answer for such an eventuality. The government, he explained, wanted their assistance in wiping out the republicans. Looking directly at the assembled group he went on to say that if any man was not up to the task he should leave the force now.

As Colonel Smyth walked along the line of policemen standing in stunned silence he stopped in front of one and asked him: 'Are you prepared to co-operate with me?' The man hesitated and then replied by saying that Constable Mee would speak for him. Constable

Jeremiah Mee, a tall man with a full moustache with waxed tips, drew himself to his full height and addressed Smyth saying, 'By your accent I take it you are an Englishman. You forget you are addressing Irishmen. You do not understand Ireland or Irishmen.' Colonel Smyth assured the group that he was in fact an Irishman from Banbridge in County Down. Constable Mee understood that Smyth was encouraging the RIC officers to shoot on sight any person they suspected of being in the IRA, an incitement to murder for which they would be guaranteed immunity by the government. Then taking off his cap and belt and laying them on the table, he said, 'That's my answer … These too are English. Take them as a present from me and to hell with you, you murderer.'

Smyth, not used to being addressed by a subordinate in such a manner, immediately ordered that Mee be arrested. District Inspector Flanagan and Head Constable Plover escorted Mee out of the dayroom to the kitchen. No sooner had they reached the kitchen than there was a stampede, led by Constable Thomas Hughes, as he and the other constables rushed into the kitchen. Mee was dragged and pushed back into the dayroom with one constable shouting, 'if a hand is laid on our spokesman again this room will run red with blood'. To their surprise, the dayroom was empty. Smyth and his fellow officers had adjourned to the District Inspector's office to assess the situation. While in the office, Smyth attempted to put through a telephone call, but the line had been disconnected. His immediate reaction was 'There are Shinners out there. They have cut the wires.' He looked out of the window and could only see a few soldiers at the Crossleys. The others had gone to various pubs for some refreshments while they waited. The thought must have crossed his mind that he and some of the most high-ranking officers in the country had been lured into some type of trap. He was, however, reassured by the number of soldiers and policemen who were in the town.

Meanwhile in the barrack room Mee, on behalf of his assembled colleagues, wrote a note, which they all signed, in which the entire group accepted responsibility for Mee's words and actions and indicated that they would resist Mee's arrest even to the point of bloodshed. Then, ignoring Smyth, one of them handed the note to the Inspector General. Another tense period followed while the officers considered this note. General Tudor, who had arrived in full dress uniform, emerged from the District Inspector's office having changed into a brown tweed suit. He adopted what today would be known as the 'good cop, bad cop' tactics. In a complete contrast to Colonel Smyth's no-nonsense address to the men, General Tudor spoke softly, adopting a conciliatory tone. He explained that the men could expect an enhanced pension if they remained in the RIC and complied with the present orders. A number of promises and concessions were made, but Mee was of the opinion that Tudor's apparently calm demeanour was merely a mask and reckoned that the promises made were worthless. Mee rejected the proposal and commanded his colleagues to dismiss them. The constables went into the yard at the back of the barracks and in defiance sang *A Nation Once Again* and *Wrap the green flag round me boys*. They confirmed that there was no turning back and returned to the dayroom. Once again the room was empty. Smyth, Tudor and the other officers along with the police and soldiers had gone. They had left for Tralee.

Unfazed by the reaction he received in Listowel, just over a week later, on the evening of Sunday 27 June, Colonel Smyth delivered a similar message to the RIC in Milltown, south of Tralee. He again arrived dressed in full military uniform with his medal ribbons on display. Such was the haste of his appointment that he had not had time to be fitted for an RIC uniform. He ordered the station sergeant and his six constables to the barrack dayroom. There he repeated the message that he was responsible to no man in Ireland and reported directly to the prime minister. Placing his revolver on a table he explained to the RIC men how their role was to change. They would in future act as scouts for the Black and Tans and would be responsible for identifying Sinn Féiners in their district. The older policemen regarded this as just another order from the top brass and felt they would find a way around it to see out their days in the force and get a pension. One young policeman was more aware of the serious nature of the order and said that when he joined the RIC, he had not anticipated shooting anyone. Behind the remark was probably the knowledge that if he went about identifying neighbours as Sinn Féiners he was liable to be shot himself. Colonel Smyth replied that times were changing and that he sounded like a coward. Taking up the line used by General Tudor in Listowel, he said that RIC men who were prepared to serve through these difficult times would be awarded big pensions. After about an hour in the barracks, Colonel Smyth once again moved on.

The Listowel policemen decided that the incident, from their point of view, was far from over and that there would certainly be repercussions later. Fearing that a large military force would be despatched by Smyth to arrest them they no longer felt safe in the barracks. They left to hold a meeting in T.D. Sullivan's public house. It was decided to commit what Colonel Smyth had said to them to paper, with a view to placing it in the hands of the press in the event of action being taken against them. Surprisingly there was no immediate retaliation by Colonel Smyth. However, fourteen single men decided to tender their resignations and the authorities were immediately notified. One of these officers, John McNamara, had said that he would be prepared to stay on, but would only perform the duties he had been recruited to do. The following day, he was summoned to appear before a court-martial, but demanded a civil trial instead.

The next morning a high-ranking military officer arrived at the barracks and told him that he had been dismissed and ordered him to leave the barracks at once. McNamara did not believe the matter would rest there. Fearful that he was to be made the scapegoat for the mutiny it was decided that the record of Smyth's speech should be made public. The document was taken in the first instance to the local curate, Father Charles O'Sullivan. On reading it, he immediately understood its political significance and suggested that it be sent to IRA headquarters in Dublin. The detailed account of Smyth's speech was then passed on to James Crowley, who was the elected Sinn Féin member for North Kerry. Crowley, anticipating the reaction that the publication of the comments might provoke, made sure that a typed copy was taken to Dublin by car without delay and presented to the *Freeman's Journal*. The following day the first edition carried the story, but subsequent editions were suppressed. A full account of the Listowel incident was printed on 10 July and the 'Listowel Mutiny' as it became known, was public knowledge, as was the 'shoot on sight' policy espoused by Colonel Smyth on behalf of the British government.[14]

Following the publication of the speech, Colonel Smyth was instructed to report to the Irish Office in London for a meeting with Prime Minister Lloyd George. He met with Sir Hamar Greenwood in Dublin and briefed him before travelling to London. In a damage limitation exercise, Smyth denied that the article in the *Freeman's Journal* was accurate. During question time in the House of Commons on 14 July the Irish Nationalist MP from Liverpool, T.P. O'Connor, raised the matter of the speech at Listowel. Sir Hamar Greenwood responded on behalf of the government, saying that he was satisfied that the newspaper report of the speech was a distortion and a wholly misleading account of what had taken place. The speech was later read in parliament and was the subject of a debate. When it was read during the debate, unionist politicians cheered each time the shooting of persons was mentioned.

It was during this visit to London around 12 July that Colonel Smyth met with Brigadier General G. Walker. In conversation with the Brigadier General he confided that he found his work in Ireland much more nerve-racking than the war, saying that he did not think his life was worth five minute's purchase.[15] Smyth later denied that he had urged reprisals and denied that he had declared that martial law was to be introduced. He also said that the only grievance the RIC men had related regarded their transfer from Listowel to more dangerous areas in Kerry. Colonel Smyth sued the editor and managing director of the *Freeman's Journal* for libel for publishing the allegations made by Constable Mee. The case, however, did not come before the courts.

The publication of the speech had a major impact on the RIC and over the next three months over 1,000 men resigned from the force rather than be party to such a policy. This was a serious setback, especially for the Black and Tans who were such recent recruits from England. Their lack of local knowledge – of individuals who might pose a threat, and even of the countryside roads – would be a major factor in reducing their immediate effectiveness.

Among the many RIC men who resigned was Jeremiah Mee. In September that year Mee, supported by Dáil Éireann, opened a bureau to help those RIC men who had resigned to find work. On 27 November he attended the Convention of the Self-Determination League of Great Britain which was held in Manchester and announced that he hoped to place 100 men in employment in England. However, the slump in English trade and industry became more acute around that time and he was not only unsuccessful – many Irish workers already working lost their jobs. His efforts met with little success.[16] Jeremiah Mee and the many RIC men were not the only people to resign as a result of the Listowel speech. Captain Chadwick, who had been present along with Smyth when he addressed the RIC men in Listowel barracks, resigned his commission in July that year.

Colonel Smyth was now a marked man. Michael Collins had been made aware of Smyth's speech soon after it was made. He realised the embarrassment that the revelation of the official British policy in Ireland would be to the government and the political mileage that could be gained from it, particularly in America among the Irish-American population. He also realised that Smyth posed a significant threat to the IRA. Instructions went out to track down and execute Colonel Smyth.

5

The Murder of Colonel Smyth

Seán O'Hegarty, acting commander of the No.1 Brigade of the IRA in Cork, knew that the County Club on the South Mall, Cork. was frequented by high-ranking military officers and senior government officials. This impressive building extended from the South Mall along Crane Street out to Phoenix Street and, as a gentleman's club, it also provided residential accommodation. The staff was considered to be loyalist and so the IRA found it very difficult to obtain information about the club and those who visited it. However, this changed when Seán Culhane, intelligence officer of B Company of the IRA's Cork No.1 Brigade, made contact with Ned Fitzgerald, known as 'Bally', from Conamore, Ballyhooley in County Cork. He was a waiter at the club and Culhane persuaded him to provide information about club members, among them Colonel Smyth. It was revealed that he had a room in the club and had stayed there during the first fortnight in July but had been away for a few days and was due to return at the weekend. The IRA, acting on the instructions of Seán O' Hegarty, set about planning an attack.[1]

On the evening of 17 July the Colonel was having a Saturday night drink at the club with a few friends. It had been a hectic week and he was relaxing with RIC County Inspector Craig, Mr Barber, the club's secretary, and another club member in the smoking room. At around 10.30 p.m. he was writing a letter to the Naval and Military Club, Cambridge House in Piccadilly, London (he had previously given his address as 96 Piccadilly West. The Naval and Military Club, also known as the 'In and Out' was at 94 Piccadilly) about a suitcase he had left behind on Thursday in his haste to catch the Irish mail train to Holyhead and from there the boat to Dún Laoghaire. On his return from London he had travelled across the country to Tralee to make arrangements regarding the holding of the Assizes and from there to Cork, again to make similar arrangements, to ensure that the Assizes were suitably protected both internally and externally from possible attack.

As he enjoyed his pipe and a drink, over a dozen IRA men quietly entered the building. While some stood guard at the door, John O'Connell, Seán Culhane, Seán O'Donoghue, Daniel 'Sandow' O'Donovan, Cornelius O'Sullivan and one other man made their way upstairs to the smoking room. The men burst into the room shouting 'Where is he?' and on recognising him shouted 'Hands up!' before opening fire, shooting him in the face, forehead and neck. Despite these wounds it was claimed that Smyth sprang from his chair, automatically reaching for the revolver in his hip pocket, rushed towards the hallway but after a few steps pitched forward, clutched the wall and slumped to the floor, dead.

Another version of events is that one of the men walked up to Smyth and said: 'Your orders were to shoot on sight. You are in sight now so make ready', after which he was shot a number of times. Both versions are unlikely to be true. The young men who carried out the attack were in an unfamiliar location and would have been high on adrenalin. Their objective would have been to shoot their victim without giving him any time to react and it is extremely unlikely that they would have paused to make a statement, however brief. The fact that County Inspector Craig was wounded in the leg during the attack tends to confirm a degree of panic in the shooting. The timing of this murder was planned to coincide with finishing time of a film in the nearby assembly rooms Picturedrome. As the assailants, who had not bothered to disguise themselves, ran out of the club, they mingled with the crowds emerging from the cinema and made their escape.

An inquest into Colonel Smyth's death was scheduled in Dublin for 19 July and sixteen jurors were summoned to attend. On the day, however, only nine attended. A police constable was tasked with persuading the others to attend, but when he returned he informed the court that each person had made an excuse. Without the required number of jurors, the inquest did not proceed and was abandoned.

The murder of Colonel Smyth in a city on the south coast of Ireland was to lead to further deaths and destruction on an unprecedented scale in the north of Ireland.

6

Colonel Smyth's Funeral

It was decided that Colonel Smyth would be buried in his parents' native town of Banbridge, County Down, in the north of Ireland. Gerald had been only ten years old when his father died and had been particularly close to his mother's side of the family, so much so that he used Ferguson Smyth as his surname. The arrangements were to transport his body from Cork to Banbridge by rail. However, the engine drivers in Cork refused to man the train which was to carry his coffin. There had been an ongoing campaign by railway workers, particularly on the southern part of the rail network, to refuse to co-operate with the military; they refused to man trains carrying munitions or soldiers. In the north, Catholic railway staff who supported this policy often faced intimidation and threats to their lives from fellow railway employees. Many railwaymen were dismissed for failing to man trains. The rail system, the key transport system in Ireland, was at this time also subject to frequent IRA mail robberies and this was generally referred to at the time as the 'Railway Crisis'.

Colonel Smyth's body was initially taken to the military hospital at Victoria barracks in Cork. On 20 July an impressive funeral service, conducted by Rev. Dr Brooks, chaplain for the forces in Cork barracks, was held in the barrack square. A massive oak coffin, placed on a gun carriage, was drawn into the square by six black horses with white trappings. Three sides of the square were lined by companies drawn from the Hampshire and South Stafford regiments as well as a detachment of fifty men from the RIC under the command of County Inspector Maunsell. District Inspector Heggart was also in attendance. After the service the 'Last Post' was sounded and the coffin was transferred to a military motor ambulance for the journey to Dublin. The ambulance was accompanied by a military escort to ensure the journey to the military hospital in Dublin was unimpeded.[1]

The following morning, on 21 July, his remains were taken from Dublin to Banbridge by train. His body was accompanied by his uncles Stanley and Norman Ferguson, by James W. Murland and his cousin, Captain Warren Murland, and senior RIC officers. The train steamed into Banbridge station at 11.50 a.m. and was met by members of the Smyth and the Ferguson families. The coffin was offloaded from the guard's van and was borne by employees of Edenderry factory to the hearse, which then proceeded to Clonaslee House on the Lurgan Road, the home of Norman Ferguson. The funeral took place later that afternoon from Clonaslee House and the local press reported that the funeral procession was one of the largest ever seen in the country. A special train from Belfast brought mourners as well as fifty members of the RIC, accompanied by their band, to Banbridge. Many RIC officers and men from barracks throughout the area also attended. One hundred men of the 1st Battalion Bedfordshire and Hertfordshire Regiment, who were stationed at Newtownards, were also present, along with the regiment's band.

At 3 p.m., the service was conducted by Rev. H. Macpherson of Guelph, Ontario, Canada, a relation by marriage of the deceased. The Macphersons were in County Down and had been staying in Warrenpoint after visiting their son's grave in England. He had been killed in a flying accident at Cambridge while serving with the Royal Air Force. The coffin, draped in the Union flag, with Colonel Smyth's service cap and sword belt on top, was placed on a gun carriage drawn by two black horses. Before leaving for the cemetery his sixty-five year old mother Helen placed a single wreath on top of the coffin as a final farewell to her son. As the funeral cortège left Clonaslee House, a line of troops opposite the driveway stood with arms at salute and later fell in at the rear of the procession. Under a clear blue sky the cortège made its way to the cemetery as the Seapatrick church bell tolled at one-minute intervals. All the local linen factories had closed as a mark of respect, as well as practically every shop in the town. In private houses the blinds were drawn. Flags were flown at half-mast. The entire route to the cemetery was lined with mourners and curious onlookers. The townspeople of Banbridge were joined by hundreds of others from the surrounding countryside. Many gathered at the 'cut', the main vantage point, to look down as the funeral procession made its way through the centre of the town to the cemetery. It wound its way along Church Street, Bridge Street and up the hill to the Newry Road before turning right into the cemetery. Among those who filed behind the gun carriage were Major General H.H. Tudor, CB CMG, commander of the 9th Division and police advisor, Brigadier General Sir G. Hacket Pain, KBE CB (divisional police commissioner for the north of Ireland), Major Leathes (Belfast) represented Brigadier General Carter Campbell, CB DSO (commander of troops in Ulster), Lt Colonel Ritson, Mr J.F. Gelston (commissioner of police, Belfast) Sir Robert Liddell and Lt Colonel W.J. Alien, DSO DL MP, on behalf of the Ulster Unionist Party. Many other officers were also present. Missing from the group of chief mourners was Major Osbert Smyth, Colonel Smyth's brother. He was stationed in Egypt and was unable to attend the funeral.

One of the many wreaths carried in the cars that accompanied the funeral was from County Inspector Craig, who had been in the club when Colonel Smyth was murdered and had been shot in the leg himself during the attack.

Colonel Smyth's body was laid to rest in the family plot alongside that of his father, as thousands looked on in silence. It was broken by three volleys of shots being fired over the coffin and by the mournful sounding of the 'Last Post' by the buglers of the Bedfordshire and Hertfordshire regiment. The grave was later marked by a tall, white, stone Celtic cross and would be the final resting-place of a father, mother and their two sons. Some time after this his army colleagues erected a plinth at the side of the grave with the following inscription:

Sacred to the Memory of Gerald B. Ferguson Smyth DSO, Brevet
Lieut. Colonel Royal Engineers
Killed 17 July 1920
Erected by those of the 9th (Scottish) Division who served with him
in France 1914 – 1918.
To perpetuate the memory of a most gallant and able officer and a
devoted comrade in arms whom they knew and loved.

7

Banbridge Riots

Many of those who had come into Banbridge to witness the funeral stayed in town, and the public houses that re-opened after the service did good business. The murder and murderers would have been the main topics of conversation. Early in the evening the streets seemed normal, but as dusk descended, crowds began to gather and it was evident that trouble was developing. A large crowd gathered in Church Square and attacked a young man named Ward, the son of a local publican, as he was cycling home. He was beaten up and his bicycle smashed. By midnight more people had assembled in Bridge Street, where they sang loyalist songs and then paraded through the streets, shouting and singing, frightening their Catholic neighbours. The mood of the crowd turned sinister when passing motorcars were stopped and petrol from spare cans was demanded. They were unsuccessful in obtaining petrol, but that did not prevent them from achieving their objective: a Catholic-owned newsagent's shop in Bridge Street, owned by Miss Mary McMahon, was attacked by between fifteen and sixteen men. The front door and the shop window were smashed and material in the window set on fire – the entire building was burned to the ground.

It was later claimed in the *Northern Whig* newspaper that an 'attempt' had been made to burn the shop because the blinds had not been drawn and it had not closed during the funeral. Prior to the funeral, on the evening of Tuesday 20 July, a specially convened meeting of Banbridge Urban District Council had been held for the purpose of passing a resolution condemning the 'dastardly and cowardly' murder of Colonel Smyth. A further resolution had been passed requesting that all businesses should close for the duration of the funeral. It was only after McMahon's had been well and truly set ablaze that the fire brigade was called out to save the adjoining property.

The next day, Thursday, the dignity and solemnity that the town had shown during the funeral had totally changed. The highly charged atmosphere following the overnight violence, coupled with the anti-Catholic feeling generated at that time of the year, particularly by the Twelfth of July demonstrations, was a recipe for trouble.

The anti-Catholic feelings had, to some extent, been generated by IRA activity in the area. In May the vacated RIC barracks in nearby Laurencestown had been burned to the ground by a party of masked and armed men. At 2 a.m. all the telegraph and telephone wires in the area had been cut and, using petrol, paraffin and hay, the group had set fire to the building. The event was witnessed by local residents Mr Gibson and the railway-crossing gatekeeper, both of whom were ordered not to interfere.

In June there was a more serious, albeit botched, attack by the IRA on the barracks in Crossgar, also in County Down. Newspaper reports that 200 or 300 Sinn Féiners had carried out the attack in the early hours of Tuesday 1 June alarmed Protestants in the county. The attack was led by Hughie Halfpenny from Loughinisland.[1] Following the usual pattern of cutting telegraph wires and barricading approach roads to the village with trees, field gates and anything else that came to hand, the armed and masked men began their attack. They broke into the homes of Michael Morrison and Robert Dickson on either side of the barracks, which were part of a terrace in Downpatrick Street. The noise alerted the RIC officers in the barracks and Sergeant Fitzpatrick and Constables Carey, Collins, Murphy, Ramsey and Wilkie grabbed their rifles and took up positions at the steel-shuttered and sand-bagged windows of the two-storey barracks.

Meanwhile, the IRA men were drilling holes in the adjoining walls of the barracks to place explosives in them. The police frantically sent up distress Verey lights, lighting up the whole area. On the opposite side of the street the IRA had taken possession of a house that happened to be Constable Wilkie's home. From there they opened fire on the barracks. Residents in the street, awakened by the noise, peered cautiously through their windows at the battle that was taking place in the street. The steady gunfire resulted in Sergeant Fitzpatrick being seriously wounded in the chest and Constable Carey being grazed by a bullet. The plan to blow up the barracks had gone very wrong. The gelignite that had been placed in the walls had not been properly tamped, with the result that when it was detonated the explosives blew back, causing minimal damage to the barracks but blowing out the windows in the adjoining houses. As daybreak approached, two hours after the attack had started, the IRA made their escape on bicycles, leaving behind their sledgehammers, crowbars, gelignite, tow, petrol and a sprayer. It was not until around 9 a.m. the following morning that Sergeant Fitzpatrick was evacuated and taken by a lorry to the county infirmary. He had been due to retire after a full period of service a few weeks' later.[2] It was incidents like this that increased sectarian tensions in the county.

Even before Colonel Smyth's funeral there had already been a sectarian attack on a Catholic family in the town land of Moneyslane, outside Banbridge. Property owned by a Mr P. Smith had been attacked on four successive nights before it was eventually looted, set on fire and totally destroyed. Speaking about the attack at Banbridge Rural District Council, Councillor Maginnis said that it was certainly not a very edifying spectacle to see the Union Jack, which was supposed to be the symbol of civil and religious liberty, floating over the remains of a Catholic merchant's property, placed there by a mob of so-called 'law and order loyalists'. He went on to say that the police barracks was within two miles of the place and no move had been made by the police to afford Mr Smith any protection. In response, Mr Stanfield said that the police were in a state of terror and were afraid to venture out of their barracks. A claim for £16,500 compensation was later lodged with the council.

The loyalists of Banbridge had ushered in the historic month of July with midnight drumming parties, the deafening sound of Lambeg drums echoing throughout the town. The conservative King William Street and Seapatrick flute bands accompanied the drumming parties as they made their way through the main streets of Banbridge. Huge bonfires were lit on Scarva Hill and Smyth's Hill. These loyalists would have attended the Twelfth of July demonstration at Rathfriland, where up to 400 Orange lodges listened to the welcoming speech by the Master of Rathfriland District Bro. John Bradford. Referring to the appalling state of things in Ireland he declared that the Church of Rome was behind all the trouble and urged every Protestant to join the Orange Order.[3] Just over a week later the celebrations and sense of superiority had changed. Despite the fact that few, if any, of the loyalists of Banbridge would have known Gerald Smyth or his family as anything other than major employers in the district, his murder was seen as the murder of one of their own. There was a mood for revenge.

On Thursday, at the start of the early shift at the Banbridge Weaving Company on the Rathfriland Road Protestant employees demanded the removal of the 'Sinn Féin' workers, i.e. Catholic workers, as they were no longer prepared to work with them. Colonel Smyth's mother had made it known that she no longer wanted Roman Catholics to be employed in any of the factories associated with her family. The factory manager at the Banbridge Weaving Company had no option but to suspend work for that day. The Protestant workers, led by bands, then went to other factories and encouraged their co-religionists to make the same demands. The result was that these factories also stopped work. Protestant workers from all the factories, estimated at around 2,000 and headed by the Seapatrick Flute Band, marched around the town mid-morning carrying Union flags and singing loyalist songs such as 'Dolly's Brae' and 'Kick the Pope'.

During the afternoon the crowd continued to chase Catholic workers from their places of employment. Police later estimated that around 3,000 people were on the streets. That afternoon Mr Faughan, a Catholic post office employee, who had taken part in a one-day strike in favour of the Mountjoy hunger-strikers, was dragged from his workplace by men claiming to be members of the UVF. (The strike was a twenty-four-hour protest in the form of a general strike against the treatment of Sinn Féin hunger-strikers in Mountjoy jail. It received widespread support everywhere, with the exception of the north of Ireland.) The police, who were at the scene, were vastly outnumbered and made no effort to prevent the attack. He was forced into the street at gunpoint and was made to walk at the head of the mob to serve as an example. He had to hobble along, humiliated, as he had lost a shoe in the struggle.[4] He was taken by the mob to his lodgings, accompanied by a police constable to ensure that he did not come to any further harm, and ordered to leave Banbridge. The policeman later denied that the clerk had been kicked or struck or had a revolver pointed at him. The man himself, however, later recalled how the mob had surrounded the Post Office and called him a 'Fenian'. He recalled how one of the men, armed with a revolver, had entered the sorting room and said 'I will take his body out'. He confirmed that he had been beaten while escorted by a police constable and was later abandoned when the police constable felt he could no longer protect him.

During the day many Catholic homes were attacked and their property looted. The McColl family house was looted and young

McColl received a gunshot wound. Many Catholic families started to leave the town.

At 2 p.m. John Somers, an engine driver with the Great Northern Railway, brought a goods' train from Newcastle into Banbridge station. John was known to have Sinn Féin sympathies and made no secret of his support for the party. On arrival he was taken from the footplate of his engine at gunpoint, bundled into a commandeered motor car and taken away. It is unclear what exactly happened to him, but when it was discovered that he was a Protestant he was released and ordered not to return to Banbridge.

There was a lull when the protesters returned to their homes for dinner, but in the evening the procession was re-formed and the streets were again crowded with people singing loyalist songs and chanting anti-Catholic slogans. Three Orange bands now joined in the procession through the town. They made their way to a field on the Lurgan Road, where a meeting, at which Mr S. Crookshanks presided, was being held. A resolution was passed by the mill workers pledging not to work alongside Roman Catholics who refused to take an oath that they would not in any way associate with Sinn Féin. The crowd returned from the meeting on the Lurgan Road accompanied by the Orange bands; Mr Crookshanks urged them to refrain from damaging property.

His appeals went unheeded. While individuals were attacked and old scores settled, violence took hold during the evening and night. Even though the local RIC was outnumbered, no call was made for military support. While there is no evidence that the police actively participated in the burnings and destruction, there is evidence that they passively agreed with it, mingling with the mob. No prosecutions would be brought against those engaged in the attacks on persons and property.

The crowds, now really a mob, attacked the Catholic-owned businesses in the town, paying particular attention to the Catholic-owned public houses, places where they would previously have been happy to have a drink. Thomas Smyth's pub in Bridge Street had its window smashed and whiskey looted. David Warnock's shop in Bridge Street did not escape either: the large plate glass window was smashed and tobacco, cigarettes, pipes and sweets were stolen. Local businessman Michael McGrath fared worse, as his shop and home at 32 Bridge Street were destroyed by fire. Francis Boyle's drapery shop had its window smashed and practically the entire stock looted. Further down at 51 Bridge Street at Patrick Coll's public house, the two plate glass windows facing onto the street were smashed. The premises were broken into and the interior fittings, including large ornamental mirrors, were broken to pieces. Cases of whiskey and other spirits were carried out the door and shared among the mob. Thomas B. Wallace, a solicitor at 36 Bridge Street, had his front window broken as the mob made its way along the street.

Premises in Scarva Street came under similar attacks. A large household furniture and boot and shoe shop in Scarva Street, owned by James Bryson, was burned. The mob made their way from street to street, systematically attacking Catholic-owned property. In Newry Street Peter McGivern's public house had all its seventeen windows smashed. The pub was looted and wrecked. Henry Mooney's tobacconist's shop was also damaged and all of the stock stolen. Another public house to come under attack was the Crystal Bar owned by James Browne at 28 Newry Street. Everything, from the plate glass mirrors to the cash register, was smashed, and the stock of alcohol looted. In a shop run by Miss Boyle in Newry Street, the windows were smashed, the front door broken down and shop fittings destroyed. A woman called Annie Kinney also had her windows broken.

Another Catholic individual who came in for particular attention was Daniel Monaghan. He had been a Sinn Féin candidate at the recent Poor Law elections and had a house furnishing business in

Scarva Street. The Monaghans were well known in the town as Sinn Féin supporters. The previous year (1919), on Sunday 5 October, a number of Sinn Féin supporters had been holding a meeting and encountered opposition from loyalists. They were attacked and a fracas developed. The police arrived on the scene and when the crowd refused to disperse the police fired shots in the air. James Monaghan, Dan Monaghan's son, was arrested by the police and taken to the police barracks. On Monday, as Monaghan was being removed from the barracks to be brought to Belfast, a crowd of supporters gathered outside the barracks to protest his arrest. The presence of the crowd made it difficult for police to escort the prisoner to the waiting vehicle and it looked like the barracks might come under attack and the prisoner freed. The police fired at the Sinn Féin supporters to disperse them, but one shot struck young Joseph Coll, the son of local publican Patrick Coll, as he stood watching the commotion. He was attended to by a doctor, who found that the young boy had been critically injured. He arranged for him to be brought by motorcar to the Royal Victoria Hospital in Belfast. In commenting on the events of Sunday and Monday, the *Banbridge Chronicle* later wrote: 'Monaghan, whose activities in the interest of Sinn Féin have already earned him some notoriety and a term of imprisonment, led to an unseemly fracas in town on Monday night … Disciples of Sinn Féin would be well advised from airing their views in Banbridge.' Following the incident at the barracks, stones were thrown at Monaghan's and O'Hare's shops. Several premises in Bridge Street also had their windows broken.

The Monaghan family was sure it would be attacked. Having seen McMahon's home and business burned to the ground the previous night, Dan Monaghan was apprehensive about his safety and that of his family, so he barricaded his family inside the building. He knew that if he left, his home and business would most certainly be burned to the ground. Following the parade through the town, groups had dispersed to various parts of the town to wreck and plunder. At around 8 p.m. on that bright July evening approximately 300 to 400 people converged on Scarva Street and, having attacked other Catholic-owned premises in the street, turned their attention to Monaghan's. The police later stated that the crowd numbered about 1,000.

The mob broke into and looted Teresa Henry's public house opposite Monaghan's. Looters drank bottles of whiskey and porter on the street as the local policemen stood among the crowd and watched. While the police had been prepared to open fire to disperse Sinn Féin supporters the previous October when they gathered to hold a meeting, no such action was taken against the loyalist rioters. The empty bottles were then used to break the windows in Monaghan's shop. It appeared that preparations were being made to set the building on fire. Someone in the crowd claimed to have seen a revolver at an upstairs window in Monaghan's house. Immediately a horseshoe, that presumably had been brought along as a weapon, was thrown at the window. It hit the window sash and fell back into the street. The mob then, despite the presence of police, rushed towards Monaghan's front door and broke it down. There were shouts of 'take Monaghan out and burn him'. Another group attacked the premises from the rear. A witness later claimed that he heard shots fired at Monaghan's house and confirmed that a number of those present were armed. A number of people would later state in court that many in the crowd were in fact armed and the witness was offered a revolver himself by a member of the mob. A shot rang out, followed by two others in quick succession. The shots were fired at the crowd from an upstairs window in Monaghan's, and in the crowd a woman called Minnie Shields was shot in the shoulder. The shot narrowly missed a policeman standing in the entrance to Henry's pub, a couple of yards away from Minnie. The newspapers later speculated that the shot had been aimed at the policeman.

Minnie was simply one of the curious onlookers caught up in the occasion. She had been to choir practice with her friend Clara Pilson and had stopped outside Monaghan's on her way home to see what was going on. Young William John Sterritt, a seventeen-year-old from nearby Victoria Street, was shot in the head as he stood outside George Wilke's shop. He later died from his injuries in the early hours of 23 July. Three others, including Fred Wilson, were wounded by ricocheting bullets. The crowd scattered, stampeding to each end of the street following the shots, as Daniel Monaghan sought to protect life and property.

To commemorate the death of Sterritt, a member of the King William Street flute band, who was simply an unfortunate victim of the attempt to drive Catholic families out of Banbridge, the local Loyal Orange Lodge, Gideon's Chosen Few LOL 257, changed its name to the 'William Sterritt Memorial'. After a period of inactivity this lodge was re-formed on 8 January 2000, retaining the latter name in memory of William Sterritt.

Until Daniel Monaghan fired those shots, the violence had been all one-way and there had been no retaliation from the beleaguered Catholic community. The police now requested military support. A detachment of troops was despatched from Newry and when the twenty-two soldiers arrived, armed with machine guns, it was claimed that they too came under fire by the occupants of the building – although this was later denied by Daniel Monaghan. Fire was directed at the building and the military and police forced their way into the premises. Daniel Monaghan and his two sons, Patrick James and fifteen-year-old Daniel O'Connell, surrendered and were arrested and taken to the police barracks. They were later taken to Newry under military escort.

By midnight the town was relatively quiet, but groups were still roaming the streets, sporadically breaking shop windows and looting.

At 3 a.m. a crowd gathered unobserved at the rear of Monaghan's and set it on fire, along with an entire block of buildings owned by the Monaghans. Thomas McMahon's barber shop and home, and Byrne's, a saddler, were among the businesses burned. Daniel Monaghan and his two sons were later charged with endangering the safety of an officer of his majesty's forces and three members of the RIC by discharging firearms and being in possession of two revolvers and seven rounds of ammunition. In a general court-martial held in October that year and defended by Mr Timothy Healy, KC, they were all acquitted on the charge of discharging firearms, thereby endangering of military and police. Daniel Monaghan was fined £10, to be levied on his chattels, on the charge of possessing the revolvers and ammunition. His fifteen-year-old son was fined 5s or one day's imprisonment. Daniel pointed out to the court that the fine could not be levied off his property as it had all gone up in flames.

Crowds continued to roam the streets on Friday and more Catholic families were intimidated and driven from their homes. Protestant workers in the weaving factories were incensed when they learned that young William Sterritt, who happened to be a fellow textile worker from Smyth's Weaving Company, had died as a result of the injuries he had received during the previous night's rioting. As a reprisal they wanted to clear the Catholics out of Banbridge factories. They were informed by factory managers, however, that production could not commence without a full complement of workers, which included the Catholic workers. As a compromise they agreed to return to work if their Catholic co-workers signed a statement promising to have nothing to do with the Sinn Féin movement. Workers at all the local mills were required to sign the following declaration:

I ... hereby declare I am not a Sinn Féiner nor have any sympathy with Sinn Féin and do declare I am loyal to King and country.

Further pressure was brought on employers to dismiss Catholic workers and orders were given not to employ them in the future. For some, this was not sufficient – they wanted to clear Catholics right out of town. This was a time for some to settle old scores, and many Catholic families were burned or intimidated out of Banbridge on personal grounds. Many families decided to leave for Newry and a steady stream of horse-drawn vehicles of all types, piled high with whatever household possessions could be salvaged, made their way out of the town. As they walked out along the Newry Road, they were jeered and spat at by some of their former neighbours. Not all Protestants in Banbridge supported this action – many, however, remained silent.

One person who was not prepared to remain silent and watch his Catholic neighbours being burned out was William Scott. He ran a plumbing business in the town along with the brother of William Sterritt, who perhaps had more reason than most to resent Sinn Féin supporters in the town. After William was killed another young textile worker, a Catholic named Barry, had made an inappropriate comment about Sterritt. When word got out about this a crowd went to the Barrys' house in Burn Hill in the lower part of Newry Street to burn the family out. Mr Barry, the young man's father, was at the time dying of tuberculosis, and a number of young children were also in the house. William Scott faced the crowd saying, 'it doesn't take brave men to burn out a dying man and young children'. His pleas were eventually successful and the crowd drifted away. His intervention came at some personal cost though. An Orangeman for many years, he felt he could no longer attend his lodge with brethren who were not prepared to accept one of the basic tenets of the order: 'To abstain from all uncharitable words, actions or sentiments towards his fellow Catholic brethren.' He subsequently left the Orange Order and was labelled a 'Home Ruler' by his fellow Protestants.[5]

After a tense night, calm returned to Banbridge on Saturday.

Local paper the *Banbridge Chronicle* reported that all the main streets showed signs of the wrecking and looting, principally public houses owned by Roman Catholics. Irresponsible reporting by this newspaper did little to ease tension in the town. In its edition of 24 July, reporting on the burning of Monaghan's, it claimed that 'during the progress of the fire numerous explosions took place, the flames apparently lighting ammunition and bombs concealed on the premises'. The premises had in fact been searched by the military before it was set on fire and only the weapons and ammunition had been recovered. The report gave many sufficient justification for their actions. The violence had not ceased however. James McMahon, the elderly owner of the first shop to be burned down, was attacked and assaulted as he returned to survey the ruins of his premises. In an effort to justify the arson and widespread destruction following Colonel Smyth's funeral, the *Banbridge Chronicle* in an editorial on 31 July stated: 'It should be clearly understood, in justice to the Banbridge people, that there is no campaign against religion. No violence has been directed against Roman Catholics as such. It is Sinn Féin that the people are determined to cleanse the town from. Surely all right thinking Roman Catholics will approve of this and give it their support.'

On Saturday a meeting of the Urban Council, attended by local mill owners, passed a resolution stating 'that we ask the authorities to allow the unionists to publicly provide armed guards for the protection of property and if the authorities refuse to do so that they send military to Banbridge for that purpose.' Later that evening the council held another meeting at which Brigadier General Sir Hacket Pain was present. Following this meeting it was agreed that a military force would be provided and, with the co-operation of local volunteers and the police, this should be sufficient to cope with any further developments. It was decided to form a civil guard and notices were to be posted inviting volunteers to enrol at the police barracks.

On the Monday night a large meeting of workers and their representatives was held in the Orange Hall in Banbridge. The meeting was chaired by Councillor Samuel Crookshanks. In discussing the action to be taken in relation to Sinn Féin supporters (Catholics, for all intents and purposes) he made it clear that all Sinn Féiners were to be excluded from all employment: only those who signed a declaration would be allowed to work. The rank and file at the meeting took a harder line, with a majority declaring that all Roman Catholic workers should be dismissed. Rev. Canon Kerr, a senior Orangeman, and Rev. Thomas Boyd, who also attended the meeting, brought a more measured tone to the proceedings and succeeded in getting the workers to moderate their demands. The requirement for Catholic workers to sign an agreement was allowed to stand. Rev. Canon Kerr made it clear that Sinn Féin was the enemy, and advised that the Roman Catholic community as such should not be subject to reprisals. He adopted a generally conciliatory stance at the time.

A strong military presence in the town, supported by civil patrols with members of the Urban Council under the command of former District Inspector Sheridan, eventually helped restore calm to the streets of Banbridge. Sheridan had recently retired as the RIC District Inspector and had been replaced by Major Leslie Roberts. The increased military personnel were barracked in the Temperance Hall and the town hall. However, when the military were withdrawn from the town on Saturday 14 August the attacks on Catholic-owned property began again. Military patrols were recalled and brought into the town every evening to control the situation. Banbridge Council argued for a voluntary curfew in the town and ordered that the all-night lamps be lit after sunset and that public houses close at 9 p.m.[6]

During this particular episode of sectarian violence and arson, in addition to Catholic-owned business premises being looted and burned, six homes belonging to Catholic families were totally destroyed and a further twelve partially destroyed.[7]

The violence spread to nearby Rathfriland following the Orange parade on the last Saturday in July. At 10.30 p.m. a crowd of about 200 attacked Catholic premises in the hill-top town. The *Banbridge Chronicle* reported that there had been stone-throwing as the bands were leaving and the local UVF turned up. The violence continued until after midnight and it was reported that the windows of premises owned by Dr Laverty, John McClean, Bernard Brooks, Jas Cassidy, Lawrence Downey and John McEvoy were smashed. One man was later arrested and fined 20s for rioting and inciting others to engage in rioting.

The anti-Catholic action did not end there and political unrest continued in Banbridge factories, as an entry in the minute book of the Milltown factory dated 11 August 1920 recorded:

> We have again to report a further disturbance in work caused by the action of the Banbridge workers as a whole in regard to Sinn Féin (due to the murder of Lieutenant Colonel Brice Ferguson Smyth). Owing to this we had for some time to carry on as well as we could with 18 workers short. [The firm refused to employ Catholic workers.] This is however gradually making itself right and we are this morning in a fairly good position. The small motor lorry is now in full commission and, we are glad to say, is doing good work. We are now open to dispose of three horses and have offered them for sale. Owing to the unsettled conditions in the Banbridge district we are keeping extra watchmen in the bleachgreen at night and have applied through the proper channels for a permit for these men to carry guns.

There was a further surge in violence in September following the murder of taxi driver William McDowell on 3 September. He was driving a Ford and returning from the Northern Bank in Banbridge with £1,300 in cash, the wages for workers in the massive Dunbar McMaster & Co. Ltd thread-spinning mill in Gilford. He had driven

William McConville, the firm's cashier, making his regular Friday visit to the bank to collect cash for the wages. As they made their way back to Gilford at 11 a.m. they came across a car at the side of the road at Knocknagar with the hood up and one of the wheels jacked up. They were flagged down by a couple of men standing beside the car. William McDowell stopped and got out of the car to see if he could be of assistance. The men standing by the car did not require assistance – they wanted the Dunbar McMaster payroll. McDowell was shot in the chest and died by the roadside. William McConville, who had remained in the car, later claimed that he was bundled out of the car and thrown over a low wall and down an embankment. The raiders grabbed the box containing the cash, got into their car and made off in the direction of Gilford.

The next morning the *Banbridge Chronicle* reported the incident under the headline 'Gilford man shot by Sinn Féin raiders'. News spread quickly in the district that the murder was the work of Sinn Féin, and this piece of irresponsible reporting was all that was needed to trigger further reprisals against the Catholic population. An armed crowd, headed by the Hope Temperance Orange Order flute band, visited every mill in the district in order to evict every Catholic still in employment. William McDowell had been a member of Hope Temperance LOL 1678. The Catholic workers remaining in Messers C. Blane and Son, Banford Bleach Works and Hazelbank Weaving were the first to go. The sackings had a domino effect and spread from the mills in Gilford and Laurencetown to Portadown where thirty-four Catholics were expelled from a hem-stitching works.

It was only a short time before Head Constable Stokes from Banbridge arrested unemployed thirty-two-year old Billy Conlon and charged him with murder. Conlon, an American citizen, had previously worked in America as a bartender. William McConville, the firm's cashier, was also arrested. Other arrests soon followed. Head Constable

Stokes brought Hugh Rodgers from Sixmilecross in County Tyrone and Frank O'Boyle, the owner of a motor garage from Beragh, also in County Tyrone, into custody. Both were reported as being common criminals involved in car theft and in selling on cars whose appearance had been changed.

When the case went to trial at the Winter Assizes in Belfast on 15 December, Conlon was found not guilty based on circumstantial evidence. The crown was not satisfied with this outcome and ordered that all the accused be tried by court-martial, something usually reserved for political offences, although there was no mention of any political motive in the murder and robbery. The subsequent trial at Victoria barracks in Belfast in April 1921 left many unanswered questions and was full of inconsistencies. All the accused presented alibis for the time and date of the murder, with the exception, of course, of the cashier William McConville. McConville had been charged with 'misprision of felony' because he had concealed information that he could have given to the authorities. It turned out that he knew Conlon, who lived in Gilford just as he did, and that he had earlier failed to identify him as one of the men involved in the murder. He had also claimed that he had been pitched over the wall by two tall men with revolvers. Conlon was 5¾ feet, Hugh Rodgers 5 foot 5 inches and Frank O'Boyle 5 foot 6 inches.[8] All of the accused pleaded not guilty at the court-martial. Conlon, Rodgers and O'Boyle were found guilty and sentenced to penal servitude. McConville was found not guilty and the charges dismissed. The suspicion of guilt, however, hung over him for the rest of his life.

The story did not end there. Conlon, O'Boyle and Rodgers featured in the headlines again in May 1927 when they, along with a fourth man, made a dramatic and well-planned escape from Belfast's Crumlin Road jail.

At no time during the trials was it alleged that there had been Sinn

Féin involvement in the murder and robbery on 3 September, but the damage had been done by the headline in the *Banbridge Chronicle*. It was not long before the expulsion of Catholic workers moved beyond the linen trade to other sectors. It was reckoned that 1,000 Catholics in the Bann Valley were expelled from work. They had to rely on subsistence-level unemployment benefits, with larger families having to seek support from the White Cross funds. The unemployed had to make their way to the Ministry of Labour office in Banbridge three times a week to 'sign on'. For those in the outlying districts this could be a six-mile walk to and from the 'bureau'.

In 1921, when there was a demand for extra workers, the Ministry of Labour sent some of these experienced expelled workers to apply for the vacancies. The loyalist workforce in these factories continued to refuse to accept Catholics unless they were prepared to sign a statement declaring that they were loyal to king and country and not members of Sinn Féin. With no other source of income available, many signed and returned to work. There was, however, no exception made in the Brookfield and Edenderry factories controlled by the Smyth and Ferguson families. 'Catholics need not apply', was the rule. It was not until the Second World War, when officers from the Smyth family served alongside Catholic officers and men also prepared to lay down their lives for their country, that the ban on Catholic employees was lifted.

On 4 October 1920 the local Orange Lodge 518 was renamed the 'Colonel Smyth Memorial'. Rev. Canon Kerr, district chaplain, conducted prayers at the inauguration of the renamed lodge (this particular lodge is no longer in existence). Prior to the Twelfth of July celebrations in 1921 the Hope Temperance Lodge was renamed the 'McDowell Memorial Temperance LOL 1678' and a new banner bearing a portrait of William McDowell was unfurled in Gilford Orange Hall.

8

Dromore Riots

The nearby town of Dromore did not escape the violence. On the night of Friday 23 July an estimated crowd of 500 gathered in Market Square and set out to attack Catholic-owned homes and businesses. The crowd's intention was clear when a shot was fired in the direction of Burns' house. The single policeman in the square, Sergeant Barton, advised the crowd to go home, but was ignored. The crowd moved to Ardery's Corner and up Gallows Street. Sergeant Barton made his way to the barracks to get support. He returned to the streets with Constable Mannion to find that the situation was rapidly spiralling out of control, with buildings being set on fire. Back in the barracks Sergeant Barton had requested military support and been promised that a military detachment would arrive in Dromore at 8 p.m. As midnight approached and there was still no sign of the military, he decided to take his remaining three constables from the barracks and provide them with rifles. The group of policemen moved to the Catholic church to protect it from being attacked and set on fire by the mob, and Sergeant Barton ordered his men to fire into the air to frighten the mob away from the church, which they succeeded in doing. At Ferris' in Gallows Street Barton fired his revolver into the air and again the crowd scattered. The police continued with this tactic, as it appeared to be the only effective means of scattering the crowd. The crowd regrouped, however, and turned its attention from burning Catholic property to attacking the police. In the crowd thirty-year-old Wilfred Henry Mitchell, a member of the Royal

Black Preceptory and the Orange Order, from the townland of Drumaknockan, was shot dead at the corner of McQuaid's Row. Dr S.B. Carlisle was called and pronounced Mitchell dead and his body was then taken to Cowan-Heron Cottage Hospital in Dromore. At a later inquest it was claimed that Mitchell had been hit in the head by a ricocheting bullet that had been fired from a .303 rifle and this was substantiated by a bullet mark on the wall close to where Mitchell had fallen. It was determined that the bullet had been fired by the police.

Sergeant Barton and his men eventually withdrew to the barracks for their own safety. The military, twenty men from the Somerset regiment, finally arrived in Dromore around 12.15 a.m. and, with fixed bayonets and supported by the police, charged the crowd and cleared the streets.

During the rioting in Dromore a number of houses were set on fire, including the home of James McCarten, an oil merchant in the town. It was claimed that his son had fired on the crowd. Around midnight the mob attacked the Pioneer Temperance Society, which was used as a Catholic club in Dromore. The club, a converted coach-house attached to the parochial house, was pelted with stones and other missiles, set on fire and burned to the ground. The crowd then turned its attention to the parochial house and began another attack. Father O'Hare, the parish priest, and his housekeeper had to flee for their lives having been ordered out at gunpoint. To show that they meant business the armed attackers shot the priest's dog.[1] The two sought protection in the home of Patrick Fitzgerald, JP, which was in turn attacked. The crowd then gained entry to the parochial house and began to systematically smash the furniture and anything else they could find.

A meeting of Orange leaders was held in Dromore on Saturday evening in the home of John Graham, the District Master. They were concerned that a member of the Orange Order had been shot by police during the previous night's riots and wanted to take over control of security in the town from the police and military. The District Master put a proposal to the police that members of the Comrades Club – former soldiers – keep order in the town, provided the police and military were completely withdrawn and confined to barracks. This was agreed to and all was quiet on Saturday and Sunday night.[2]

On Monday morning a meeting between the town's publicans was held in the town hall and it was decided that public houses would be closed until 9 a.m. on Wednesday and every night of the remainder of the week from 6 p.m. On Monday girls from the local factories, also closed because of the unrest in the town, paraded through the streets carrying a Union Jack and chanting that all Catholics should be put out of the factories.

9

Lisburn Riots

On the night of Saturday 24 July, Lisburn was relatively quiet until a group of ten to fifteen men marched, in formation, to the corner of Railway Street and Market Square. A large crowd soon gathered in Market Square, as reported in the *Lisburn Standard*, to show their anger at the murder of Colonel Smyth. At about 10.30 p.m., at the corner of the Northern Bank, the men in formation sang a few verses of the well-known Orange song *Dolly's Brae* (the song celebrated the success of the Orange Order in a provocative march though a Catholic area in County Down and the subsequent clash with Catholic 'Defenders', in which up to thirty Catholics were killed). The crowd enthusiastically joined in the singing and when it stopped a call went up: 'Come on boys let them have it'.

The crowd then moved *en masse* to Linenhall Street and the Central Hall, owned by the Lisburn branch of the Ancient Order of Hibernians, an exclusively Catholic organisation. The hall had previously been a Methodist chapel and was an impressive building located between James Hanna's blacksmith forge at Smithfield and a row of thatched cottages which adjoined the Damask factory at the corner of Market Lane. Only the caretaker, known as 'Yankee Bill', was in the hall and he faced the crowd alone, saying that he would thrash any man who would take him on. There were no volunteers – instead the crowd, armed with stones, attacked the building, breaking the vaulted windows facing onto Linenhall Street. The attack was so ferocious and the noise of the breaking windows sounded like gun fire. Shots had not in fact been fired, but rumours immediately spread that there had been a shooting at the Hibernian hall. The police attempted to maintain some semblance of order, but as the whole police force in the town numbered only fourteen men it was an almost impossible task. The crowd, realising that all the available police in the town were in narrow Linenhall Street, rushed back to Market Square, where an orgy of destruction of Catholic-owned shop windows began, unimpeded by any kind of police presence.

With shouts of 'Down with Sinn Féiners' the crowd then rushed to Gilmore's shop and house at Cross Row, Market Square, which they attacked. Gilmore's had been singled out because Mr Gilmore, a member of the local Board of Guardians, was a Sinn Féin supporter. The home of Dr Clarke in Seymour Street also came under attack. The police later regrouped and drove the crowd out of Market Square and into Bridge Street, as it appeared that premises were about to be set on fire. They called for military reinforcements, but were informed that the military were not in a position to respond. Catholic-owned public houses as far away as the County Down Arms on the Hillhall Road were all singled out for attack. Those who suffered damage and in most cases looting included: Hugh Rice, Hillhall Road; Thomas Caldwell, Bow Street; Peter McKeever, Bridge Street; James Neeson, Smithfield; Harvey and Maxwell, Market Square; John McKenny, Bow Street; Michael McKenny, also Bow Street; Owen Trainor, Longstone Street; Quinn and Downey, Chapel Hill; Lucy McFall, Bridge Street; Henry Connolly, Market Square; Daniel Mooney, Chapel Hill.

However it was not just Catholic-owned public houses that suffered. The window of Jellie's, a Protestant public house, was also broken. Harvey and Maxwells, also a Protestant-owned pub, it was reported, suffered accidental damage during the bombardment of Connolly's pub, which was next door to it in Market Square. It was

Quinn and Downey's public house and grocery shop on Chapel Hill that suffered most from the looting. Christmas came early for the looters when twenty gallons of whiskey, thirteen bottles of brandy, thirty dozen bottles of stout and fifteen dozen bottles of ale were stolen. The compensation claim that followed detailed that the grocery shop had been cleared of stock and that even the cash register was stolen. The two large plate glass windows of Michael O'Shea's china and hardware shop in Market Square were also broken and a large quantity of stock destroyed. The convent of the Sacred Heart of Mary on Castle Street, occupied by a community of twenty-eight nuns also came under attack and twenty-seven of the windows facing the street were smashed. At 3 a.m. the crowds began to drift home and an uneasy calm descended on the town.

This was not the first time the convent had come under attack. Established in 1870 by ten French nuns from Béziers, with Mother St Thomas Hennessey as superior, they planned to hold a fundraising bazaar in the nearby town hall in October 1872. There had already been sectarian riots in Belfast that August, following protests by the Orange Order to prevent a nationalist demonstration in support of Home Rule. This had raised religious tensions in the town and the Protestant community in Lisburn objected to the nuns using the town hall. At the request of local councillors the nuns changed venue and used the convent instead. Angered that they had not been able to prevent the bazaar from taking place altogether, a mob of Orangemen occupied the town hall on 10 October, burned an effigy of parish priest Father Edward Kelly and then proceeded to attack the convent and to break up the fundraising bazaar. Only the intervention of the police and military prevented the mob from gaining access to the convent after many of the windows were broken. Only after the Riot Act was read, clearing the way for firearms to be used against the mob, did they disperse. The convent was attacked again on St Patrick's Day

1874, when members of the Orange Order classified the singing of Irish songs and hymns by children in the convent as provocative.[1] Now, almost fifty years and two generations later, latent sectarianism had once again surfaced.

The trouble in Lisburn did not end on the night of 24 July; there were further attacks on isolated Catholic homes and businesses. On 26 July stock and furniture in Bernard Doherty's public house at Ravarnette, outside the town, was destroyed by a crowd of up to twenty-five men. Later Alexander Gallagher, William Lunn, Robert Crawford, William Crawford and John Morton from Magherageery and George Glover from Ravarnette were charged – at a special court held in Banbridge police barracks – with assaulting Bernard Doherty and his wife Mary, and with the theft of intoxicating liquor. The haul from the public house included a barrel of stout valued at £8 10s, six dozen bottles of whiskey and two dozen bottles of brandy. The barrel was later found empty a mile and half away from the public house. Morton was charged with hitting Bernard Doherty between the eyes with a hammer. During the attack Mary Doherty was beaten and knocked unconscious and Head Constable Stokes, who was in charge of the investigation, later confirmed that Mrs Doherty's face was black and swollen and described it as a mass of pulp. The group who attacked the publican and his wife were prosecuted at Hillsborough Petty Sessions on 4 September and released on bail. At the Winter Assizes in October the jury acquitted Gallagher and Glover and could not agree on Morton. They were released on continuing bail to the next assizes. Bernard Doherty would later claim £130 for the damage done but Judge Matheson, hearing compensation claims, said that it was monstrous to suggest that there had been £100 worth of stock in that small country public house. He awarded £60, to be levied on the electoral divisions of Blaris and Maze. This was reported in the *Lisburn Standard* under the heading 'Bad news for Blaris and Maze

Taxpayers'. There was no mention of the attempted murder of the publican and his wife.

On the night of 26 July yet another public house came under attack. This time it was at Hillsborough, just outside Lisburn. It was wrecked and looted, and again the owner and his wife were assaulted.[2]

10

Violence spreads

While the civil unrest in Lisburn following the funeral of Colonel Smyth was undoubtedly influenced by events in Banbridge and Dromore and as far away as Bangor and Newtownards, the events that were taking place in Belfast, ten miles away, must also have been a major contributing factor.

On 11 July Sir Edward Carson and Lady Carson had attended the unveiling of Craigavon Black Preceptory's new banner at the Orange Hall in Clifton Street Belfast. In a speech that once again linked politics and religion, Carson set out what would be the theme of his speech the following day at the annual Twelfth of July demonstration at Finaghy:

> If I know my men of Ulster no majority could ever impose on them a form of government that they loathe and detest. They fought Home Rule from 1911 onwards through many vicissitudes and they organised in a way which would have made it impossible to impose this hateful thing upon them. Their brave volunteers would never have submitted, for one moment, to the yoke of Dublin Parliament governed and guided through the Hierarchy of the Church of Rome.

At Finaghy, midway between Belfast and Lisburn, the link between politics and religion was clear to every Orangeman who walked under the arch at the 'Field' with the slogan 'Rome stands today where she has always stood'. Sir Edward Carson addressed a larger audience of Orange brethren gathered at this field with the same theme: 'We in Ulster will tolerate no Sinn Féin – no Sinn Féin organisation, no

Sinn Féin methods.' He went on to make a direct threat to the British government while delivering a clear message to those listening and to those who would later read his speech in the local newspapers:

> But we tell you this – that if, having offered you our help, you are unable to help us from the machinations of Sinn Féin, well then … we will take the matter into our own hands. We will reorganise in our own defence, throughout the Province, the Ulster Volunteers and those are not mere words. I hate words without action.

To cheers from his Orange Order audience he added, 'Now I hope I have made that pretty clear'. He emphasised the size of the Orange Order, perhaps for another audience, saying that 30,000 Orangemen had been recruited in the past year.

Carson had signalled to the Orange Order that action against supporters of Sinn Féin and the Church of Rome, which to many of his supporters were synonymous, had his tacit support. He had played to the inherent sectarian element of the Orange Order and with a 'nod and a wink' left it up to working-class loyalists, fired up with Twelfth of July rhetoric, to take action. It was not long before they took matters into their own hands.

On 21 July, the day of Colonel Smyth's funeral, workers returned to work after their annual holiday, known as the 'Twelfth Fortnight'. On their return to Belfast shipyards they found notices calling Protestant and unionist workers to meet at lunchtime, which would indicate that there was a degree of planning involved in subsequent events. At the meeting a call was made to drive out all disloyal workers. Workers from the Workman Clark & Co. shipyard marched to the larger Harland and Wolff yard and ordered out all Catholic workers, as well as any socialist workers, given that Carson had warned them not to trust people masquerading as socialists. At the 'Field' at Finaghy on 12 July he had told the assembled Orangemen:

These men who come forward posing as friends of labour care no more about labour than does the man in the moon. Their real object and the real insidious nature of their propaganda is that they mislead and bring about disunity amongst our own people, and in the end before we know where we are, we may find ourselves in the same bondage and slavery as in the rest of Ireland in the South and West.

It was crucial for the unionist leadership to attack socialism. The labour movement had the potential to unite Protestants and Catholics and to erode the Protestant working-class vote. Any disunity within unionist ranks could adversely impact the unionists' negotiations with Britain, so socialists were placed on a par with Sinn Féin.

Catholic workers were driven from the shipyards and some were thrown into the water and pelted with rivets as they swam for their lives. Retaliation followed that evening as the by now exclusively Protestant workforce returned home from work. Catholics in the Short Strand in East Belfast stoned trams as they carried workers home from the shipyards. This was to be the start of what can only be described as open warfare between the Protestant and Catholic communities in parts of Belfast. The violence soon spread to other districts and the Catholic population in these areas responded in kind. Catholics were driven from all the major factories and mills in Belfast, including Mackies, Gallaghers, the Sirocco Works and Barbours. Many Catholic families were also driven from their homes. It was later estimated by a committee chaired by Catholic bishop Dr McCrory that 10,000 men and 1,000 women were expelled from work.[1] (This figure may have included a number of Protestant workers regarded as socialists.) The extreme violence in Belfast and the concerted action to intimidate Catholics into leaving their workplaces would certainly have been taken on board by loyalists and their leaders in Lisburn.

Sir Edward Carson, in his speech at Finaghy, had made reference to the Ulster Volunteers. Back in 1912 the Ulster Unionist Council had decided to use 'all means which may be found necessary' to prevent the introduction of Home Rule in Ireland – a proposal to locate a second parliament in Dublin which the Protestant and unionist population feared would give Catholics a greater say in the affairs of Ireland. The phrase 'all means which may be found necessary' was included in a pledge made by over 471,000 men and women who, in 1912, signed the Ulster Covenant to resist the efforts of the Liberal party in the House of Commons 'to place Protestant Ulster under the domination of a Roman Catholic and Nationalist Ireland'.[2]

Prior to the signing of the Covenant on Ulster Day, Sunday 28 September, Sir Edward Carson had committed to a number of speaking engagements, taking him from the west of the province towards Belfast, where he was to make a speech in the Ulster Hall at a religious service. It was, however, a religious service with a political message. Before the packed Ulster Hall Carson declared:

> We are plain, blunt men who love peace and industry. The Irish question is at bottom a war against Protestantism; it is an attempt to establish a Roman Catholic ascendancy in Ireland to begin the disintegration of the Empire by securing a second parliament in Dublin.

The message could not have been clearer. He had visited Lisburn on 18 September and had reviewed a huge parade of men carrying wooden dummy rifles in a torch-lit procession. They were accompanied by Orange bands with fifes and drums playing *The Boyne Water* and *The Protestant Boys*.[3]

The UVF was established with men who had signed the covenant. They initially trained with wooden rifles, but that all changed when, in April 1914, tons of arms and ammunition were clandestinely imported at the ports of Bangor, Larne and Donaghadee and, with military precision, swiftly transported to prepared dumps throughout

Ulster. In Lisburn, before 1914, the Lisburn battalion of the UVF had access to 200 guns and this number and the quality of arms would have increased considerably post-1914.[4] After April they were equipped with uniforms and new armaments that included machine guns and an ample supply of ammunition. Despite the fact that this was an illegal army, the encouragement offered by leaders such as Sir Edward Carson and, indeed, the strength of the UVF, gave the ordinary Protestant confidence that they were untouchable by the government. Training was conducted on a regular basis and in Lisburn the drill hall, a large building in Graham Gardens, proved inadequate, so a mill at Sprucefield was requisitioned because it seemed to be the ideal location. The immense rooms and sheds at the mill, all secured behind high walls, were ideal for drilling, shooting and storing arms. Ownership of the premises many years later transferred to the Royal Ulster Constabulary.

The Lisburn contingent of the UVF consisted of nine companies comprising almost 1,000 men and known as the 1st Battalion South Antrim Regiment. It was under the command of Adam P. Jenkins and among the officers were Edwin A. Sinton, Edward Smyth, E.S. Clarke, J.H. Davies, William Megran, A. Woods, George Duncan, Joseph Lockhart, James Lowry, William Gordon, James Carson, Cecil Ewart, William Wilson, Robert Brown, Walter C. Boomer, George Wilson and B. Leonard. The unionist women of Lisburn also played their part. A large first-aid class under the instruction of Dr George St George was formed by the South Antrim Women's Unionist Association and a new branch of the Ulster Volunteer Ambulance Corps was inaugurated under the command of Mrs Edwin Sinton.

It must be asked why members of this force did not assist the police and the military in stopping the violence in Lisburn on the night of 24 July. A meeting of the UVF was held in Lisburn Orange Hall on the following evening and Captain Alex Woods, a former RAF officer, was appointed commander, while Sergeant Major Braithwaite was appointed assistant commander in charge of the County Down side of the town. That evening, after nine o'clock, four citizen patrols went on duty on the streets of Lisburn and 'co-operating with the police prevented further destruction of property'. The claim that they were co-operating with the police was somewhat disingenuous: the Royal Irish Constabulary was predominately Catholic (and a number of constables in Lisburn were Catholic), so the loyalist view was that Catholics were allied to Sinn Féin and could not be trusted. The objective in 'co-operating with the police' was in fact to reduce the power and influence of the police. Wilfred Spender had been asked by Sir Edward Carson on 16 July to resign from his job at the Ministry of Pensions and to take the lead in reforming the UVF. Spender later claimed: 'All intelligence work in Londonderry and Tyrone and I think, Fermanagh is now being done by the UVF in direct communication with the military, the RIC being eliminated completely.' On 30 July the UVF placed the following advertisement, under the heading 'UVF', in the *Lisburn Standard*: 'A meeting will be held in the Orange Hall, Lisburn this Friday evening at 8 o'clock to enrol members for the above force. All those enrolled are requested to attend. J.A. Woods'.

This resurgence and reorganisation of the UVF, known as Carson's Army, was happening not just in Lisburn, but across the north of Ireland. Sir Edward Carson had argued that although the northern counties were relatively peaceful, the IRA's campaign would move steadily northwards, and he mentioned recent attacks on RIC barracks in Ballynahinch and Crossgar as cases in point. He claimed that if the pattern in southern Ireland, where small RIC barracks were abandoned if deemed too difficult to protect, was repeated in the north, the Protestant population and property in many areas would have no protection from the IRA. Military resources were already stretched to the limit fighting a guerrilla war in southern Ireland, so there was little hope of military support for the police in the north. In some rural areas groups of vigilantes began to appear and, using their own arms, they would guard against strangers coming into their districts.

One of the main advocates of this policy of Protestants helping to protect their own areas was Captain Sir Basil Brooke in County Fermanagh. He had lobbied Dublin Castle to support the creation of a Special Constabulary, but while in principle there was support for citizens to assist the police, the carrying of arms was not permitted under any circumstances.

It was not only in rural areas that vigilantes organised themselves. Rev. John Redmond, rector of St Patrick's Church of Ireland parish in the Ballymacarrett area of east Belfast, was appalled at the actions of his co-religionists following the expulsion of Catholic and socialist workers from the shipyards. They had looted and burned Catholic-owned shops, pubs and houses on the Newtownards Road and had evicted Catholic families from their homes. In the midst of alcohol-fuelled anarchy, many took advantage of the complete breakdown of law and order to also loot Protestant-owned property. However, it has to be said that Rev. Redmond did not shed many tears at the destruction of Catholic public houses and spirit grocers. A vociferous campaigner for temperance, he regarded public houses as 'the ruination of many women and homes' and claimed that the owners were 'nearly all Roman Catholics who were regarded, not without some reason, as Sinn Féiners'. He also took the view, widely held in the Protestant community, that when loyalists went off to join the 36th Ulster Division to fight in the war, Sinn Féiners took their well-paid jobs. The result was that those loyalists who had survived the horrors of the war had no job to return to and had to go on the dole.

The widespread violence in this part of the city included an attack on St Matthew's Catholic church at the corner of Bryson Street and the Newtownards Road. Only the intervention of the military, firing shots over the heads of hundreds of rioters, saved the church. The mob nevertheless returned the following night to attack the convent next to the church, occupied by nuns of the Cross and Passion Order. Armed men broke into the building and sprinkled petrol over furniture in two rooms. The rooms were then set on fire with little concern for the nuns still in the building.[5] Again it was only through the intervention of the military that the nuns were saved from the blazing building. Catholics from the nearby Short Strand area had gathered to protect the chapel and convent from attack, and fierce fighting ensued. The only option open to the military was to open fire on both sides.

In Belfast, only three days after the violence erupted, seven Catholics and six Protestants met with violent deaths.[6] In the ensuing days crowds believed to number up to 10,000 patrolled the main streets of east Belfast to protect their area against any incursions by the Catholic population.

It was in these circumstances that Rev. Redmond invited ex-servicemen, who included UVF members, to a meeting in Albertbridge Orange Hall to discuss how what he considered the rabble element, often drunk on looted alcohol, could be controlled. His view was that the ex-servicemen would be sufficiently disciplined and capable, given their military experience, of controlling the loyalist crowds on the streets, together with the police force. He was successful in recruiting a sufficient number of volunteers and they took to the streets marching in formation and taking up position at shops or other premises that were under threat. The crowds on the streets were less likely to attack members from their own community and the presence of these volunteers did have a calming influence. The Reverend also led by example and when a Catholic mob from the Short Strand launched an attack on Protestant workers, he stepped between the opposing factions, at some personal risk, and was successful in persuading the Catholic mob to withdraw. On 26 August the Redmond Volunteers, who were organised to control the loyalist mobs in east Belfast, were enrolled as special constables in the school attached to St Patrick's church. When the Ulster Special Constabulary was officially sanctioned in November that year, many of the original volunteers signed up to join the new force.

It has been claimed that the creation of the Ulster Special Constabulary was a spontaneous reaction by the Protestant community in Ulster to attacks by the IRA on the Royal Irish Constabulary. In east Belfast, as in Lisburn, the special constables were in fact created to control the wilder elements of rampaging loyalist mobs. Following November 1920 the role of the special constables changed, when they did indeed come under attack by the IRA, and many officers, genuinely committed to defending their communities, paid with their lives.

While the original vigilante and volunteer groups had been established for different purposes – to protect rural areas from incursion by the IRA, and in the city to protect lives and property within Protestant areas – they were preparing the way for politicians to implement a more ambitious plan. Carson and Craig had plans to create a legally armed force over which they, not Dublin Castle, would have control. The plan was now taking shape. Over the coming months and years there would be a blurring of lines between the membership of special constables and the UVF.

11

More violence in Lisburn

In Lisburn six men arrested during the Saturday night riots on 24 July appeared before a special court held in Smithfield police barracks on Sunday afternoon. Five local men were released on bail to appear before the next Petty Sessions. A man with a Belfast address was remanded in custody for trial later in a Belfast court. The Lisburn Petty Sessions, with William McElroy presiding, was held on 5 August. Patrick Campbell, Market Lane; Hugh O'Kane, Sprucefield; James Coulter, Bullick's Court; William Carlisle, Millview and Samuel Chapman were charged with offences related to the rioting on 24 July. All pleaded guilty and only Samuel Chapman was represented by a solicitor, W.G. Maginess. Chapman, he said, had a wife and four young children and had no previous convictions. He had not broken Quinn and Downey's window, but was drunk, so when the window was broken 'whiskey bottles were staring him in the face and he stole some bottles'. Maginess asked the court to take a lenient view. DI Swanzy, prosecuting, agreed that the court should take a lenient view, saying, 'In these particular cases I think if your Worships put the defendants under a rule of bail it would do more to keep the peace in Lisburn than anything else. That is merely a suggestion.' The chairman responded that the cases were very serious from the ratepayers' point of view, and asked if the Inspector thought there was any danger of a recurrence of the trouble, to which Swanzy replied that he did not think there was the least danger. Little did he realise that his own death within the month would culminate in sectarian violence of unimaginable proportions in Lisburn. The chairman said that the magistrates had considered sentencing each defendant to six months imprisonment, as they deserved it, but in view of the suggestion by DI Swanzy each defendant would be discharged on condition that each entered into a recognisance of £10 and two sureties of £5 each. The defendants were all released on bail to keep the peace and be of good behaviour and to abstain from intoxicating liquor for the next two years. The decision of the court did not give the Catholic population of Lisburn and the businesses which had suffered over £7,000 of damage in a single night much confidence.

DI Swanzy, by influencing the verdict of the court to ensure that the culprits, all of whom had pleaded guilty, did not receive a custodial sentence, was in fact giving a clear signal to those who had little respect for law and order. The burning and looting of the shops and homes of Catholics was, in his view, of little consequence.

On the morning of 19 August Swanzy attended a presentation in the Magistrate's room in Lisburn courthouse to mark the promotion of his predecessor, District Inspector Gregory. The event had been planned for 22 January, but Gregory had been engaged in duties in Counties Cork and Kerry, and the presentation was postponed. At the presentation of an engraved plate, which was attended by – among others – resident magistrates and council officials, Swanzy made a speech thanking Gregory for his work in Lisburn over the previous ten years. In response, Gregory painted a glowing picture of a peaceful Lisburn free from serious crime. He neglected to mention the murder on 9 June that year of Jane Carlisle, a mill worker from Gregg Street who was thrown into the River Lagan by her former boyfriend John McNair after a row about her ending the relationship. He said that during those ten years there never had been any conflict between the police and any section of the community in Lisburn. While this may have been true, it was a strange comment to make following sectarian rioting that had taken place in the town only a month earlier. He was in fact reinforcing for his audience of fellow loyalist and Orange brethren the stance taken by Swanzy following the riot – that such action would not lead to any conflict between the police and the Protestant and loyalist people of Lisburn. By the same token he was confirming that the Catholic community in Lisburn had not caused the police any problems over the previous ten years. He went on to say that he hoped that DI Swanzy's stay in Lisburn would be very happy and pleasant; Swanzy would not live to see the end of the month.

12

Planning to murder Swanzy

By this time Michael Collins' order to find DI Swanzy was well underway. Collins had taken the murder of his friend Tomás MacCurtain badly and had written to Terence MacSwiney, who later succeeded MacCurtain as the lord mayor of Cork, saying, 'I have not much heart in what I am doing today thinking of poor Tomás. It is surely the most appalling thing that has been done yet.' His intelligence service had been asked to give top priority to finding Swanzy, but none of the many informants within Dublin Castle were able to provide details of Swanzy's whereabouts. Even Ned Broy, a confidential typist at the detective division headquarters in Great Brunswick Street, Dublin drew a blank. It was not until the information about Swanzy's initials being found on luggage to be forwarded to Lisburn eventually flowed through the IRA's communication system that they discovered his whereabouts. It was, however, one of the numerous informers within the RIC, Sergeant Maurice (Matt) McCarthy, a Kerryman stationed in Chichester Street barracks, Belfast, who passed on the information confirming that DI Swanzy was due to take up a post in Lisburn. Collins had no hesitation in authorising his assassination.

The extent of IRA intelligence operations at the time, and their contacts within the RIC, were demonstrated by their ability to track DI Swanzy to a temporary posting in Downpatrick. He had taken charge of the County Down RIC prior to taking up his post as District Inspector in Lisburn.[1] The order to assassinate Swanzy was passed to the Northern Divisional Headquarters and to Joe McKelvey, leader of the IRA's 1st Battalion, Belfast Brigade. He delegated the task to Hughie Halfpenny from Loughinisland, leader of the IRA in Downpatrick, which was somewhat surprising as Halfpenny was due to be demoted within the IRA. This may have been as a result of the failed attempt to blow up the barracks in Crossgar in June and the fact that the active service unit spent so much time at the scene, exposing the whole unit to possible capture. The IRA men under his control, however, rallied around him and refused to undertake the assassination unless he was allowed to retain his rank. Presumably McKelvey agreed to this, as preparations were made to assassinate Swanzy.

A member of the IRA in Downpatrick had daily access to the RIC barracks in Irish Street and was able to monitor Swanzy's movements. When it was discovered that Swanzy was due to leave the barracks alone at a certain time one night, the plan to shoot him was set in motion. On that wet and windy night a lone IRA gunman took up position in a doorway halfway down Irish Street, with the intention of shooting Swanzy as he walked past. The wind had extinguished a nearby streetlight and that gave the IRA man, hiding in the shadows, more confidence. At the appointed time the door of the barracks opened, but three officers emerged. They all had their overcoat collars turned up and their heads bowed to protect themselves from the wind and rain. The IRA man was unable to recognise his target and was not prepared to take the risk of opening fire on three RIC officers. The three men made their way down Irish Street oblivious of the man in the doorway and his murderous intent.

When news of this failed attempt reached McKelvey it did little to enhance Hughie Halfpenny's reputation. It most certainly did not impress Michael Collins in Dublin. Considering the Downpatrick IRA incompetent, and with the assassination of Swanzy a prime objective, he looked around for experienced IRA men and turned to the men of Cork No.1 Brigade, who had recently murdered Colonel Smyth. They, without hesitation, volunteered to take on the task.

A team of five men who had previously reported to Tomás Mac-Curtain was formed. They were Seán Culhane, Dick Murphy, Leo (Stetto) Ahern, C. McSweeny and Jack Cody.[2] Culhane, a shop assistant, was the brigade's intelligence officer and he took the lead. He knew Swanzy by sight, as the officer had visited the shop at the arcade in Cork where he was serving an apprenticeship. He requested the job of killing Swanzy himself. Culhane would later recall how he (and Florrie O'Donoghue, Cork Brigade Adjutant) had travelled to Dublin, with the train fare to Belfast in his pocket, to meet Michael Collins, Cathal Brugha and Richard Mulcahy in Vaughan's Hotel. The group discussed how to assassinate Swanzy and when asked how he proposed to carry out the attack, Culhane replied that it was a very simple little job. Cathal Brugha responded 'My God, a simple job!' Culhane later admitted that he was extremely nervous in Collins' and Brugha's presence and that his heart was in his boots as he expanded on his answer. He refused to smoke as he was afraid that his hand holding the cigarette might shake. He said that the best thing would be to shoot Swanzy in the street and have a getaway car parked near-by. Collins took a personal interest in the plans to assassinate Swanzy and diplomatically questioned Culhane's ability to take on the job. Culhane later recalled:

> I met Mick Collins and, after a frank discussion, he remarked that the job was much too big for me. I probably looked immature as at the time I was not yet twenty years of age. Collins said it was a job for experienced men and mentioned about picking selected men from Dublin. I made a strong protest to him and informed him my orders were very emphatic and that it was to be solely a Cork brigade job. After thinking it over he said he would leave the decision to the Minister for Defence [Cathal Brugha]. The Minister questioned me very closely as to my proposed

plan of action, which I fully explained to him. After many questions Brugha relented and said, 'Alright go ahead boy'.

Collins then instructed Culhane to get in touch with Matt McCarthy, the RIC informant in Belfast, as well as Joe McKelvey. He said that McKelvey was a good kid and that Matt would give him all the information he needed about Swanzy.

Having agreed that Culhane – who had participated in Colonel Smyth's murder – would have to liaise with the IRA in Belfast and seek their help with Swanzy's assassination, the Cork men realised that their distinctive accents might arouse suspicion, so collaboration with locals was essential. It would appear, given the choice of Belfast, that the IRA did not have a presence in Lisburn. Joe McKelvey was contacted and invited to come to Dublin to discuss plans to assassinate Swanzy. Discussion centred on whether the Belfast team or the Cork team would take the lead in the murder. Joe, a seasoned and leading IRA man in Belfast, offered to do the shooting, but Culhane was adamant and said that he was under instruction from Seán O'Hegarty, commander of the Cork No. 1 Brigade, that it must be a Cork job. Joe protested but eventually gave in.

A meeting was later arranged with nineteen-year-old Roger McCorley who was the OC of the 2nd Battalion Belfast Brigade and one of the leading IRA men in the city.[3] Seán Culhane, Dan O'Donovan and Jack Cody travelled by train from Cork to Belfast to make arrangements to kill DI Swanzy. Cody, a fair-haired eighteen-year-old, had been brought along as a driver.[4] Culhane stayed at the home of Joe McKelvey, who lived with his recently widowed mother Rose at 26 Cyprus Street in the Falls Road area of Belfast. It is thought that all the Cork men also stayed there.

Culhane later met with Matt McCarthy, who was in uniform, in Kearney's public house. McCarthy confirmed that he had been told that it was to be a Cork job, but that the Cork men would need a lot of help from Joe McKelvey, and that a daily report on Swanzy's movements would be required.

Seán Montgomery, who later documented the activities of those involved in the republican movement in Belfast in the 1920s, gave an account of how the operation proceeded:

> The Lord Mayor was murdered in Cork by an RIC gang led by DI Swanzy and H.C. Ferris. After the murder of the Cork man DI Swanzy was sent to Lisburn for safety and Ferris was made DI and posted to Springfield Barracks, Belfast. We, the Belfast brigade, were ordered to make arrangements to find out how to get at them. The OC [Joe Mc-Kelvey] was visiting Lisburn and took up a seat in Lisburn Park on Sundays. He was there to find out what time Swanzy left for church. On Sunday the OC was in the park, he must have been seen too often. The DI himself came over to him and asked what he was coming to sit there for; he answered he came there to see a girlfriend who was in service in a house and she had let him down for the last three weeks – the DI told him to go home and forget about her. A report was sent to general headquarters in Dublin with the result that two Cork men arrived in Belfast and reported to Belfast headquarters.[5]

This account by Montgomery presupposes that Swanzy had been identified for Joe McKelvey before he undertook the reconnaissance mission. It is possible that the Downpatrick IRA had provided a description, or that Sergeant Matt McCarthy, who had confirmed Swanzy's posting, had obtained a photograph of him. McCarthy had previously obtained a photograph of Inspector W.C. Forbes Redmond for Michael Collins. Redmond had spent fifteen years as a detective in Belfast before being appointed second commissioner of the Dublin Metropolitan police and tasked with reorganising G Division, which had responsibility for investigating political crime. He also was on Collins' assassination list.

Joe McKelvey was not the only one to keep DI Swanzy under surveillance. Seán Culhane recalled that there were two 'scouts' and one of them was Tom Fox, who lived in Durham Street, Belfast. Fox later became a colonel in the pro-treaty Irish Free State Army. Roger McCorley later recalled that Culhane and Joe McKelvey cycled to Lisburn to inspect the area. They had obviously spent a number of days staking out Swanzy's movements, but there may have been an element of bravado in Montgomery's account of DI Swanzy approaching McKelvey in Lisburn Park. The only park where McKelvey could have had sight of those going into Christ Church Cathedral was Castle Gardens on Castle Street and it would have been necessary to stand on the street to see people crossing from Railway Street to the cathedral. At that distance a person would need to be well-known to be identified. As Swanzy lived in Railway Street he would have had to go out of his way to approach McKelvey as he made his way to the cathedral. In any event, McKelvey had discovered that Swanzy had a set pattern on Sunday mornings. Sunday 15 August was the date set for Swanzy to be murdered.

On Sunday 15 August a telephone call was made to a Belfast taxi firm to book a taxi for a journey to Portadown via Stoneyford, outside Lisburn. The caller gave the name of a well-known man in the Shankill Road and asked for the driver to pick up the fare at the corner of Tennant Street in Belfast at 11.45 a.m. This was a deliberate ploy by the Belfast IRA men to give the name of a man from a Protestant district, and the destination and route were to loyalist areas.

Taxi driver George Nelson, who was a former army sergeant from Bright Street, Belfast, stopped at the corner of Tennant Street to pick up his fare. He confirmed later that four young men got in and repeated the instructions to take them to Portadown. They asked him to travel by way of the Springfield Road to Stoneyford and then take the road to Portadown. The unsuspecting driver headed up the Springfield Road. He recounted that he was well past Hannahstown when three masked men emerged from a hedge and levelled revolvers at the car and called on him to halt. As he brought the taxi to an abrupt stop, to his amazement his passengers put on masks, produced guns and got out of the car. He was ordered to climb through a gap in the hedge, where he was blindfolded and his hands were tied. As he was being led away he heard the car starting and being driven away. Jack Cody was the driver. Nelson was taken some distance away to a barn, where he was held captive by two men. He could hear them talking, but they spoke in low voices and he could not make out what was said. However, when another man joined them Nelson was able to catch part of the conversation, including that the newcomer was to be relieved at 6 p.m.

After a period of prolonged silence Nelson gathered that he was alone and managed to free himself and remove his blindfold. As he made his way out of the barn he found himself on a deserted hillside. He walked across a number of fields until he came to the main road – the road he had driven up before being ambushed. As he walked back towards Belfast he came to Charlie Watter's public house near the junction of the Hannahstown Road. The pub was situated on the hillside above the level of the road, with a commanding view of the countryside and on the narrow lane leading up to the public house he found his taxi. It had been damaged, with the floorboards pulled up and the wiring disconnected, no doubt the work of Jack Cody. He managed to make some temporary repairs, but was unable to get the engine started. He was, however, able to release the handbrake and let the car roll down the steep incline to the main road and across it to the equally steep Hannahstown Road. He allowed the car to freewheel down Hannahstown Hill towards Belfast and succeeded in getting to the bottom of the Glen Road where he finally stopped at the tram depot. He contacted his firm and another taxi was despatched to tow his car back to the taxi depot.

There are varying accounts of what happened when the taxi was hijacked. One states that the car broke down and the plan had to be abandoned. The other account is that the would-be assassins did not find their victim in Lisburn. There is, however, every likelihood that Cody, from Cork, got lost in the maze of side roads north of Lisburn. The mission was in any event postponed and the Corkmen, with the exception of Culhane and Murphy, returned to Dublin.

Plans were made to make another attempt to assassinate Swanzy. This plan was similar to the previous one and again involved the use of a taxi. On Sunday 22 August a telephone call was made by a 'Mr Brady' to the Belfast Motor Cab & Engineering Company at 47-55 Upper Library Street, Belfast, for a taxi to collect a fare at the Great Northern Railway station on Great Victoria Street, Belfast. The taxi was booked to take a run along the County Down coast. This time the taxi driver, Seán Leonard from Bedeque Street, was aware of the real purpose of the journey. The IRA had learned from the mistakes made in the previous attempt and had selected one of their own men as the driver. The plan was for twenty-eight-year old Leonard from B Company to claim later that his taxi had been hijacked.

As Leonard made his way from the taxi depot at the corner of Library Street and Upper Library Street through the city centre to Great Victoria Street, Roger McCorley was already in Lisburn. His job was to monitor Swanzy's movements that morning. At the railway station Leonard picked up Seán Culhane, Dick Murphy and Belfast IRA man Tom Fox and drove the ten miles to Lisburn. The plan had been to murder Swanzy as he made his way to church from his home in Railway Street. Joe McKelvey had previously been given the task of finding out the time Swanzy went to church. The assassins, however, got their timing wrong and were late arriving in Lisburn.

It was quiet in the centre of Lisburn when they arrived, as Sunday services were taking place in the town's churches. Leonard turned the car so that it was facing towards Belfast and parked outside a

Dr Campbell's surgery between the town hall and the Technical College on Castle Street. A car parked outside the doctor's house, with the engine running, would not attract too much attention. The three passengers and the driver got out of the taxi and sauntered down Castle Street, past the Co-operative Store and towards Market Square. Roger McCorley was already waiting anxiously in the doorway of Boyd's chemist shop at the corner of Railway Street and Castle Street. All were respectably dressed for a Sunday morning and did not attract any attention. McCorley confirmed that Swanzy was in the cathedral and would pass Boyd's shop on his way home for Sunday lunch. He told them that it would be about an hour before the service was over. Despite the risk of being challenged by a passing police patrol they decided to wait. Seán Culhane later recalled that he found that the hour passed very slowly. With revolvers at the ready they waited for the congregation and their victim to emerge from the cathedral. There were two exits from the cathedral, but either one would bring Swanzy past the spot where they were standing. The gun that Culhane had brought along had particular significance – it had belonged to Tomás MacCurtain. It was the gun that had been hidden in the baby's cot on the night he was murdered. The permit for the gun had been signed by Swanzy in Cork in the mistaken belief that it was for a loyalist in Cork city. The 'loyalist' was Jim Grey, a car mechanic who was transportation officer in the Cork No. 1 Brigade. The IRA had set him, his brother Miah and young Jack Cody up in business as automobile engineers in a garage across the road from the gate to Cork's Victoria military barracks. This was an ideal vantage point to monitor the comings and goings at the barracks and even provided opportunities to gain access to vehicles inside the barracks – in order to repair them. The gun was obtained on the pretext of protecting Grey and his business from possible attacks by the IRA. It was then passed to MacCurtain.

13

The Murder of District Inspector Swanzy

That Sunday morning, 22 August, DI Swanzy had been in the office at Railway Street barracks. Sergeant Francis Rourke was on duty and had been chatting to him around 11.30 a.m. It was just a normal Sunday in Lisburn, but that was to change. Swanzy had left the barracks and was off duty when he attended Sunday service at Christ Church Cathedral. Just after 1 p.m. he was making his way towards Railway Street and his home. The morning service at Christ Church Cathedral at the top of Market Square had just finished and the congregation was filing out of the church. Some were walking through the narrow gateway, flanked by tall stone pillars, between Gilmore's tobacconist and confectionery shop and Ferguson's shop to the Square and others used a side entrance that took them directly onto Castle Street. The area outside the church was soon filled with men and women dressed in their Sunday best. Groups stood chatting before heading home for Sunday lunch. No one paid any attention to the well-dressed men who were standing chatting in the doorway of Boyd's chemist shop at the corner of Railway Street, opposite the Northern Bank. DI Swanzy exchanged pleasantries with Major G. Valentine Ewart who, along with his father, Frederick William Ewart, had just left the church. They did not notice the men leave the Boyd's shop doorway and cross the crowded street. As Swanzy and his friends turned the corner at the Northern Bank the four men came from behind, pushed Major Ewart and his father into the doorway of the bank, produced a revolver and shot Swanzy in the head. The shot was fired at point blank range by

Seán Culhane, hitting Swanzy, as he later claimed, behind the right ear and exiting on the other side of his head, between his ear and his eye. Almost simultaneously, Dick Murphy, the other Cork man, fired a volley at Swanzy too. As he fell, further shots were fired into his body, with McCorley pausing to deliver the *coup de grâce*.

The men ran off along Castle Street towards the waiting taxi. The sound of the gunshots caused everyone to look towards the corner of Railway Street and Market Square. There was confusion, with some men running away from the corner and others running towards it. Some members of the congregation gave chase to the fleeing gunmen, but were stopped in their tracks when McCorley turned and opened fire on them. Captain Woods, commander of the UVF in Lisburn, made a valiant attempt to stop McCorley, lashing out at him with his blackthorn stick. McCorley immediately shot at Woods and the bullet struck the blackthorn stick and went on to hit a Miss McCreight, grazing her leg. One of the other shots struck the window of the Co-operative store. Thomas J. English, clerk of the Lisburn Petty Sessions, also narrowly missed being shot. McCorley, providing covering fire for his colleagues, was now some distance behind them. As the rest of the assassins piled into the taxi to make their escape, they failed to notice that McCorley was not with them. McCorley was about twenty yards from the car when it started off. Fox was the first to realise that McCorley had been left behind and he shouted to Leonard to stop and opened his door to see what had happened to his colleague. In recounting the incident later, Fox said, 'I got out of the taxi, which was slowly moving ahead, and as I did so McCorley climbed in on the other side. The jerking of the car as he climbed in caused him to discharge the last round in his revolver which went through the seat I had just vacated.'[1] (Culhane's version stated that Dick Murphy tripped, accidentally firing his gun). Fox later claimed that they were pursued by the police in a taxi:

Bow Street, Lisburn (Mooney Collection)

Quinn and Downey public house, Chapel Street, Lisburn (Mooney Collection)

County Down Arms Hotel, Hillhall, Lisburn

Inscription on the Smyth family grave, Newry Road Cemetery, Banbridge (P. Lawlor)

Donaghy's boot factory, Graham Gardens, Lisburn (Mooney Collection)

Rioters pose for a photograph outside the gutted parochial house, Lisburn (Mooney Collection)

Market Square, Lisburn (Irish Linen Centre & Lisburn Museum [ILC & LM])

Connolly's public house, Market Square, Lisburn (ILC & LM)

McFall's public house, Bridge Street, Lisburn (ILC & LM)

Peter Tougher's shop, Bow Street, Lisburn (ILC & LM)

Owen Trainor's public house, Longstone Street, Lisburn (ILC & LM)

McKenny's public house, corner of Antrim Street/Chapel Hill (ILC & LM)

Catholic homes, Longstone Street, Lisburn (Mooney Collection)

Donaghy's boot and shoe shop, Market Square, Lisburn (Mooney Collection)

O'Shea's hardware shop and Thomas Browne's public house, Market Square, Lisburn (Mooney Collection)

McCourtney's tobacconist's shop, Bridge Street, Lisburn (Mooney Collection)

Red Cross nurse (left) pauses for a photograph in Bow Street, Lisburn (looking towards Market Square) (ILC & LM)

*AOH Hall, Neeson's and McClarnon's public houses, Smithfield, Lisburn
(Mooney Collection)*

*Market Square,
Lisburn (ILC & LM)*

*Redmond Jefferson's
store and sawmill,
Bow Street, Lisburn
(ILC & LM)*

Mooney's public house/Empire Hotel, Chapel Hill, Lisburn (ILC & LM)

McClenaghan's home, Lisburn (ILC & LM)

The police commandeered it and followed us. Our car could not exceed 30 m.p.h. while the taxi with the police was much faster. We had a good start, but must have been overtaken before long, if in going round a sharp corner too quickly, the pursuing car had not pulled off two tyres. We had been expecting that we would be pursued immediately and we had grenades and heavier arms in the car to enable us to carry out a running fight, or to meet the police on foot if the car was put out of action. After the tyres came off the pursuing taxi with the police, however, the escape was surprisingly easy. [There is no contemporary account of the police giving chase at that time.]

A crowd, horrified at what had happened, quickly gathered. Among them was Dr St George, who, as he left the cathedral by the Castle Street exit, had heard what he thought was the backfiring of a motorcycle. He saw the men running away and the crowd gathering at the Northern Bank corner and then watched the taxi speed away in the direction of Belfast. Among those who witnessed the event was a doctor's wife convalescing after an illness. On hearing the shots and the commotion outside she looked out of her upstairs window and saw the assassins take off in the taxi. She scratched the registration number on her windowsill. Another witness was W.J. Connolly, who lived at 3 Castle Street. He had also watched the fleeing gunmen from an upstairs window. He claimed that shots were fired in his direction, breaking one of the brass balls of the Castle Loan Office next door to his house. Mr Connolly was regarded by the police as a key witness and was later brought to Scotland Yard in London for protection. He lived in Scotland Yard for six months and had a police escort whenever he left the building. His family was brought over to London to visit him from time to time.[2] Other witnesses later confirmed that the car had turned left at Wallace Park onto the Belsize Road, the old road to Belfast.

Dr St George made his way down the street and saw Swanzy lying on the footpath. Swanzy's sister Irene, on hearing of the shooting, had rushed from her home and was cradling her brother's head. The doctor confirmed that Swanzy was dead and that he had probably died instantly from a gunshot wound behind his ear. He also noted blood on the right-hand side of his chest and other wounds on his left side. The time was 1.06 p.m. Swanzy was carried into Northern Bank house (the bank manager lived on the upper floor). His body was later taken to his home on a stretcher.

14

The Burning of Lisburn

News of the murder of DI Swanzy spread like wildfire throughout Lisburn town and the surrounding area. There was little doubt among the general population that this had been the work of the IRA. The shots were heard by a young Catholic boy, William McConnell from nearby Barnsley's Row. He had been watching a pitch and toss game with other children and, when he heard the gunfire, went to investigate and saw the pool of blood on the pavement outside the bank. Within half an hour a crowd had started to gather. The police had no doubt that this murder would lead to another round of rioting similar to that of 24 July. The police from the three barracks in Lisburn had proved inadequate in controlling the rioters then, so unless they had assistance there certainly would be no hope of them containing any of the expected trouble in the town now. As described previously, following the last incident members of the UVF had taken to the streets, albeit after the rioting had finished, to assist the police in 'maintaining law and order'. Indeed an advert and notices had been placed in the local newspaper following the riot about a meeting in the Orange Hall to enrol new members in the UVF. Whatever had been agreed at that meeting did not encourage individuals in the UVF to present themselves for peace-keeping duties this time.

The crowd in Market Square quickly grew in number. They condemned the murder of DI Swanzy, with the more vocal placing the blame on the IRA, Sinn Féin and their Catholic supporters. Soon Market Square was filled to capacity and a mob mentality took hold.

It was obvious that a repeat of the previous onslaught on Catholic-owned property was about to take place.

The police nevertheless attempted to control the situation and made a baton charge to disperse the crowd. But they were vastly out-numbered and completely irrelevant. A telephone call for assistance was made to the police in Belfast and a force arrived from there, under the command of Assistant Commissioner Harrison. Some of the police cars turned around immediately to give chase to the assailants' car, which by this time, of course, was long gone. The crowd, later described as numbering in the thousands, headed for Isabella Gilmore's confectionery shop at Cross Row, at the top of Market Square, beside the entrance to the cathedral. The shop had the name of the previous owner, R. Fitzsimons, over the shop front and a restaurant sign above the two upstairs windows. The windows of the shop had been smashed during the July riots; now it once again came under attack. It was claimed that Mrs Gilmore's two sons were prominent members of Sinn Féin and the mob sought revenge for the murder by attacking this family.

The front door was broken down and, frustrated at not finding anyone at home, the mob dragged every piece of furniture in the house into the street or threw it from upstairs windows and set everything alight. The fury of the attack was such that even the upstairs window frames were torn out. When the mob started to attack the shop and her home, Mrs Gilmore had to jump from a back window into the cathedral graveyard, which backed onto the house. She had to make her way to safety through what she later described as 'a howling mob who threatened to shoot her'. It was claimed that shots were fired at the crowd from the house. The police from Belfast entered the house and conducted a search, but the house was unoccupied and no arms were found. At this point the Belfast police returned to the city. At one stage during the afternoon the cathedral bell was rung – a signal for the UVF to report for duty. Fully armed men who were ready for action were soon seen on the streets.[1] The select vestry at the cathedral had, for a number of years, permitted the bell to be rung to call out the part-time firemen as the fire bell at the Railway Street fire station could not always be heard. This time the firemen were already on the streets.

As the flames from the Gilmore's furniture grew, so did the crowd. Other premises in Cross Row to face the wrath of the mob were Peter Fusco's ice cream parlour, which was wrecked and looted, and later that night Nelson's, a boot shop, faced the same fate. Like Gilmore's, Fusco's shop had already had its window smashed in the July riots. Young William McConnell, whose curiosity got the better of him, watched as the violence unfolded. He would recall, years later, that his most vivid memory was a piano crashing to the pavement having been pushed out of the upstairs window of a Catholic shop at the corner of Market Square and Castle Street. Military support for the police was requested and soldiers from the 1st Battalion Somerset Light Infantry arrived by motor lorries from Holywood in County Down. Soldiers were quickly deployed to protect the Sacred Heart of Mary convent, which had come under a sustained attack during the previous riot. After soldiers alighted from a lorry to guard the convent, the mob attacked the lorry and set it on fire.

The call went out to attack McKeever's Bar, a short distance away in Bridge Street. The bar had previously been owned by Mrs Phelan and the name C. Phelan was still over the door, but the mob was aware that the new owner was a Catholic. Peter McKeever had spent some time in America and had returned about a year previously. He had decided to invest the money he had made abroad in a public house and when he heard the crowd and the sound of breaking glass on Bridge Street that day, he and his wife secured the premises and ran upstairs to their apartment to lock away the takings from the bar. The mob once again smashed the two ornately embossed front windows of the bar, replaced following the riot on 24 July, broke down the door and rushed into the pub. It was systematically looted and wrecked. It was only about 2.30 p.m. at this point. As the mob raced up the stairs, shots were fired, some going through a window. Reports that shots had struck the building opposite McKeever's pub gave rise to allegations that shots had been fired at the crowd storming the building. In the *mêlée* the owner was shot in the right side of his chest and Dr Campbell and Dr MacKenzie were called to attend to the injured publican. The military had by this time come on the scene and were trying to provide support for an ambulance that had been called to take McKeever to the local infirmary. The mob refused to let the ambulance through and cut the tyres on an army lorry which had been brought in to help the ambulance gain access to the injured publican. A group of men pushed the ambulance down the steep hill of Bridge Street, shouting: 'Colonel Smyth didn't get an ambulance and he won't either.' It was almost three hours later, at 5.15 p.m., when Rev. J.B. Bradshaw, curate at Christ Church Cathedral, with the help of Lisburn's men's VAD corps (Voluntary Aid Detachment formed from British Red Cross Society and the Order of St John of Jerusalem to provide nursing assistance) and under armed military escort, managed to get McKeever out the back and through the cathedral graveyard. As the ambulance had at this stage been disabled, McKeever was carried to the infirmary – a relatively short distance away on Seymour Street – in a quilt. He was attended by Dr George St George and his assistant Dr A.G. Johnston. Both doctors were kept busy that day, treating over two dozen Catholics who received severe beatings at the hands of the mobs on the streets of Lisburn.[2] It was almost four months before Peter McKeever was fit to leave the hospital.

Fortified by the strength of the crowd and the alcohol looted from

McKeever's bar, the mob was now in full riot mode and it moved on to the next target, the Ancient Order of Hibernians Hall in Linenhall Street. Many streamed down the narrow Market Lane (Piper's Hill) past the Damask factory, while others made their way from Market Square via Market Street. The hall was pelted with stones and set on fire. Flames were soon billowing from the large circular window above the door of this former church. The roof caught fire and, to the sounds of crackling timbers and the cheers of the crowd, collapsed into the building. The rush of flames into the sky scattered burning embers over the thatched roofs of adjoining houses. The crowds blocking off both ends of the narrow street prevented the fire brigade accessing the building, with the result that it was not only burned to the ground, but four adjoining houses were burned out as well. Only the façade of the building survived the attack. The fire brigade was successful in saving the First Presbyterian church, which backed onto the Hibernian Hall.

As evening turned into night the rioting intensified and under the cover of darkness individual Catholic homes were attacked. One of the many attacked was that of William Shaw, a member of Lisburn Urban Council and Lisburn's only Sinn Féin councillor. Mr Shaw was dragged from his house in Haslem's Lane into the street, where he was set upon by the mob and badly beaten. All the furniture was taken from his house and piled high in the street. Despite the risk to other houses in this narrow street, which ran from Smithfield and exited via a gateway into Bow Street, the furniture was set on fire and burned. Shaw was later admitted to the infirmary. Fearful that he might be attacked in the hospital, he discharged himself a couple of days later, against doctor's orders, and was smuggled away in a car.

As night wore on the attacks continued and more and more fires lit the night sky, as property after property burned. The conflagration was visible for miles and could be seen as far away as Belfast. Catholic residents in the west of Belfast obviously viewed this with considerable alarm, as they feared that this might be part of a co-ordinated assault and that they too would come under attack.[3] The situation was completely out of control. Local Protestant clergy, including Rev. H.B. Swanzy, cousin of the murdered District Inspector, had earlier in the evening tried to reason with the rioters, but to no avail. Pleas made on behalf of DI Swanzy's mother and sister fell on deaf ears.[4]

The local police were outnumbered and assistance was sought from other towns. District Inspector Moore from Larne arrived early in the evening to help direct operations but did not have the resources to tackle the ever-growing mob. At 3 p.m. the military in the town had received reinforcements in the form of four detachments under the command of no less a person than Sir Hacket Pain. This was perhaps the worst possible scenario for the Catholic population in Lisburn. Brigadier General Hacket Pain was one of the leaders of the UVF. It was he who had given orders for the transfer of guns for the UVF from the *Clydevalley*, anchored off Tusker Rock, and provided instructions regarding the storage of weapons and ammunition.[5] As colonel and chief staff officer with responsibility for UVF headquarters from 1914, his name was at the bottom of many of the printed circulars and instructions issued to the UVF. A few weeks earlier he had walked through Banbridge behind the coffin of Colonel Smyth and had witnessed the arson and destruction by loyalists in that town following the funeral. His sympathies most certainly did not lie with Sinn Féin or their supporters. With the UVF on the streets of Lisburn he was not about to attack the force which he had helped to create. His refusal to take robust action to quell the rioting and looting gave those on the streets extra confidence to continue with the mayhem. The mob simply ignored the presence of the military and got on with the looting and burning of property.

Even a downpour of rain did not dampen the ardour of the rioters. The fire bell was sounded to assemble the volunteer firemen, but they refused to respond. The military, in addition to protecting the large convent, placed a cordon across Chapel Hill to prevent the mob reaching the Catholic church. The few police who were on duty could do little as thousands on the streets provided cover for those engaged in looting and burning. Sergeant Rourke, who earlier that day had been chatting to DI Swanzy in the Railway Street barracks, could only stand and watch as McKenny's public house in Bow Street was looted. The mob beat down the front door, swarmed into the pub and carried off whatever they could lay their hands on. He watched Henry Magee from Millbrook Road, whom he had known for years, along with others, roll a barrel of porter from the pub towards Market Square. It was just 9.15 p.m. Newspaper reporters found it difficult to get from Belfast to Lisburn by road and had to depend on the restricted Sunday railway service. A reporter from the *Irish News* wrote: 'the crash of falling masonry could be heard even outside of the town while the tongues of flame and myriad sparks lit up the sky for miles. Bow Street was a veritable inferno.'

Among those to witness the flames were Seán Culhane and Dick Murphy, on the evening train from Belfast to Dublin on their way back home to Cork. They had escaped from Lisburn 'through the hills', taking the back roads to Belfast, and made their way to Joe McKelvey's home in Cyprus Street in the Falls Road area.[6] It is doubtful that the taxi would have stopped in Cyprus Street, as it would have been unusual for residents in that area to use a taxi and would have drawn attention. The car may have been driven directly to Tate's Avenue, where Joe McKelvey was waiting to dispose of the guns used in the killing.[7] Leonard returned the car to the taxi depot at 4 p.m. Culhane's main recollection of the time he spent in the McKelveys' house was that he changed his socks, which were presumably splattered with blood – he recalled Mrs McKelvey giving him a pair of light blue socks. After a meal the two Corkmen walked down Grosvenor Road to the Great Northern Railway station, in Great Victoria Street, to catch the Dublin train. They had been in Belfast for only two hours. Despite the fact that the train was 'lined with spotters' Culhane and Murphy took their seats in the first class compartment. As the train approached Lisburn, where only a few hours earlier they had assassinated DI Swanzy, they had started to play cards. Culhane later recalled, 'on the train passing through Lisburn we noticed a number of houses on fire, which we heard later were houses of Catholic sympathisers'.[8] Following Swanzy's murder the police had set up roadblocks as far away as Banbridge, but the men they were searching for were relaxing in first class seats and passed unimpeded through Lisburn on their way to Dublin.

When the train pulled into Amiens Street station in Dublin, they mingled with the other passengers on the crowded concourse and made their way, unchallenged, down the steps from the station onto Amiens Street. They then went up the street towards Nelson's Pillar and turned right on Sackville Street (now O'Connell Street), heading for Parnell Square and Vaughan's Hotel. There they met with Michael Collins, who was anxious to hear if the mission had been successful. He asked, 'Is it done?' and Culhane replied, 'If he isn't, his shadow is'. Collins then made a quick telephone call and on hanging up shook Culhane's hand saying, 'He's as dead as a maggot – how did you get down so fast?'[9] Collins wanted to get the two men out of Dublin at once, but they spent three nights at Vaughan's Hotel before returning to Cork. Culhane, who was on 'sick leave' supported by a doctor's certificate, decided not to risk being challenged getting off the Dublin train in Cork so he got off at Blarney and made his way home from there. He was challenged anyway, by a military patrol on the street outside Peg Duggan's house, but explained that he was only out for a walk and he returned home safely.

The rioting in Lisburn continued throughout Sunday night. Individual Catholic homes and businesses were targeted by the now drunken mobs. The *Northern Whig and Belfast Post* reported that groups of youths were lying drunk in various parts of the town, with Graham Gardens a particularly popular venue for the consumption of looted alcohol. There was a lot of open space and few houses in Graham Gardens and it was relatively secluded. In nearby Bachelors Walk, Catholic homes received particular attention. Patrick Stronge, a retired publican at No. 8, Patrick Elmore, a fishmonger at No. 70 who sold fish door to door, and the Clavin family were among those in Bachelors Walk who had all their personal possessions – everything they owned – dragged from their homes and set on fire in the street. Only the fact that the houses in Bachelors Walk formed a terrace saved them from being burned. The rioters realised that there was a risk of the whole street, along with many Protestant-owned houses, being destroyed.

The same situation saved Thomas Keenan in nearby McKeown Street from losing his home, but did not prevent his furniture being carried from the house and being consigned to the fire. Attacks were not limited to Catholics living in the town. At Knockmore two fine houses occupied by Hugh McClenaghan and his son John McClenaghan, both cattle dealers, were razed to the ground, as were the outbuildings and contents of the farmyards. Bernard Dougherty's public house at Ravarnette, previously attacked in July, was looted under cover of darkness and houses in Gregg Street and the Low Road came under attack too. At 4 a.m. fires were still burning fiercely and crowds still roamed the streets.

In Dromore rioting flared once again – Catholic businesses were attacked and looting was widespread. Catherine Kearney, a spirit grocer in Meeting Street, had all the windows in her shop broken and the rioters cleared the shelves of everything they could steal. One by one Catholic shops, including the premises of David McGcown's shoe shop and Patrick Neeson's grocer's shop in Gallows Street, had their windows broken and front doors forced open. The Commercial Hotel, owned by John Mooney and also previously the subject of attacks, was again targeted. This time the mob gained access to the hotel and stole whatever they could lay their hands on. The windows in the homes of individual Catholics in Princes Street and Gallows Street were smashed as the rioters made their way through the town. On Monday morning an exodus of Catholic families fearful for their lives began. On Monday evening at 8 p.m. a detachment of men from the Royal Field Engineers, under the command of Captain Murphy, arrived in Dromore and immediately cleared the streets, returning the small town to some semblance of order. The local magistrates had held a meeting earlier in the day and issued an order for public houses in the town to close every evening at 6 p.m.

The violence in Lisburn continued into Monday. Even as the inquest into the death of DI Swanzy was taking place in the courthouse, groups were again gathering on street corners, planning further destruction. It was just midday when Henry Dornan's butcher's at the corner of Bridge Street and Market Lane was attacked and set on fire. Policemen were on duty but powerless to act because of the sheer number of rioters on the streets. Among the policemen on duty that day was Sergeant Robert Edgar. He watched as William Gilmore, 'mad with drink', and with a petrol tin in hand led a party of about a hundred people in the attack on Dornan's. Sergeant Edgar tried to reason with Gilmore, but to no avail. The fire quickly consumed the entire substantial three-storey brick building, which included other shops. Barkley Greer, 4 Bridge Street, was one of the unfortunate traders whose shops were set alight by fires in adjoining shops. Located next door to Dornan's, it too was completely destroyed. Barclay Greer, a stout man with a black walrus moustache, was well known in Lisburn and his grocery shop at the top of Bridge Street was one of the most popular in the town. He suffered a double misfortune – not only was his grocery shop destroyed, but he also owned the adjoining butcher's shop occupied by Henry Dornan. The shops were later rebuilt with the new butcher's shop window set above glazed tiles which included a painting of an ox head in the centre. The business was later taken over by Andrew Scholes.

Gilmore later faced charges of rioting and arson, and received a suspended sentence of three months. Across the street McKeever's Bar, which had been wrecked on Sunday, was set on fire. It was not long until all the Catholic homes and businesses in Bridge Street were attacked and the gangs in the street were so drunk that they cared little if other houses or shops were damaged as well. James Douglas, who owned a fruit shop, and Leo McCourtney and his family were among those who lost their businesses. McCourtney's had a large tobacconist's shop and the plate glass windows on each side of the entrance to the shop were smashed and cigarettes, tobacco and confectionery looted before the three-storey building was set on fire. The flames set the accommodation above the shop ablaze burning through the two floors and setting fire to the roof, sending slates cascading into the street. Hamilton's next door, a Protestant-owned public house with fine embossed glass windows, survived intact.

Also destroyed were the premises of J. McFall, 86 Bridge Street at the junction of Bridge Street and Back Lane, which ran uphill to the gas works. McFall's was a Catholic-owned public house and had been serving customers since 1835. Not only was it a public house, it was also home to the McFall family. The mob smashed in the small front door, looted the contents and set it on fire. All that remained was the shell of the building, the slated roof having collapsed into the blazing interior. The gable end of the building provided evidence of how fierce the fire was, with scorch marks reaching high above the side door and the three upstairs windows. The building was later demolished and the McFall family moved to a house in Back Lane.[10] The shop next door, a Protestant property, survived intact and would later be photographed with its shutters in place and a Union Jack flag hanging from one of the upstairs windows. Across the street at the corner of Bridge Street and Quay Street the 'Lagan Stores', a large, modern two-storey Protestant-owned public house that had been built at the turn of the century also remained intact. Many of the rioters were so drunk on stolen whiskey and porter that they were impervious to the risks they were taking as they stood close to buildings while brickwork collapsed into the street and slates from the roofs rained down and smashed on the street.

Among the premises destroyed on Monday was the E. Donaghy & Sons boot factory in Graham Gardens. A major employer since it was established in Lisburn in 1850 as the largest boot factory in Ireland, it was burned to the ground. One hundred jobs also went up in smoke. (Donaghy decided not to rebuild his factory in Lisburn and set about building a new factory in Drogheda, away from the sectarian strife in Lisburn. His new factory opened in 1932.) The following day, when people were poking through the still smoldering debris to see what could be salvaged, part of the charred body of a man was discovered. The fire in the factory had been so fierce that the steel girders that supported the roof were bent and twisted out of shape by the heat of the flames, so the body had obviously also been burned beyond recognition. The local coroner, Dr Arthur Mussen, who was also County Antrim Grand Secretary of the Orange Order, refused to hold an inquest, saying that an inquest was unnecessary and would be a farce as the remains could not be identified. The remains were assumed to be those of a rioter and nobody came forward to claim the body. Donaghy's boot and shoe shop at 25–27 Market Square, which had all its windows broken and was looted during the previous riot, was again looted. This time however it was set on fire and burned out. Once again only the shell of the building remained.

The evening wore on and at 8 p.m. other premises in Market Square, also previously attacked, were now also burned out. McKenny's Bar which had been attacked during the previous riots still had its windows boarded up but members of the mob armed with hatchets hacked through the boards and broke into the building and looted it. They then moved upstairs and threw furniture out of the upstairs windows into the street. Other premises attacked included Walsh's china shop, Todd's grocer's, Burn's, a fruiterer and Pelan's, the pawnbrokers, which was looted before being partly burned. Among those later arrested for the looting and burning was William George Bratty, Linenhall Street. District Inspector Moore, Sergeant Rourke and Sergeant James Kelly witnessed Bratty breaking into Burn's shop and, with the help of others, removing the stock. The contents of a petrol can were poured over the woodwork in the shop and it burst into flames. The house next door was already on fire at this time. Bratty was later arrested but the case, despite the evidence of the policemen, was dismissed as a case of mistaken identity.

Thomas Browne's public house was also set on fire. Thomas, a Catholic, originally from Clones, County Monaghan, was just twenty-nine years of age and had only recently set up business as a publican in Lisburn. He had been so proud to see his name in large letters outside his public house in a prime location in the town. Now his pub had been looted and destroyed; he was later photographed standing outside the ruined pub before starting the task of rebuilding his business. He was not the only member of the Browne family to suffer. His brother James, who also had a public house in Newry Street, Banbridge, suffered a similar fate at the hand of rioters intent on destroying Catholic-owned property in that town.

Robert Bannister, a solicitor whose offices were above two of the shops set on fire, lost all his files and books as the fires from below engulfed his premises. The only indication that his office ever existed was a brass sign that read 'R.G. Bannister' on the wall to the right of the front door. A large, round Automobile Association sign on the wall between two upstairs windows, indicating the distance to Belfast, Newry and Dublin, also survived the flames.

O'Shea's large hardware shop, damaged in the previous riots, suffered the same fate again. The fact that the family lived above the shop did not deter the arsonists. Michael O'Shea, a former RIC officer, had left the force and married a local girl Catherine Connolly. They then opened the hardware shop in Market Square that was now home for their seven children. His son, also Michael, had been staying out at Maghaberry and when he heard about the riots he made his way into town to check if the shop had been damaged. He arrived to find the shop and his home ablaze. As he made his way forward to find out if the family had escaped, he was recognised and badly beaten. He eventually made his way across the fields to the back of his Aunt Catherine's house on the Antrim Road. She was married to John Fitzpatrick, headmaster of the local Catholic school at St Joseph's Hall on Chapel Hill. There was little comfort for him when he arrived there: he found John and his wife standing outside their rented house as their furniture and personal belongings burned in the front garden. Two young boys, James Curry and William Booth, later found themselves on remand along with others in connection with the rioting and the destruction of furniture at the Fitzpatrick home.

As all this was happening there was little the police could do other than stand back and watch. They would later claim that they were powerless to stop the mob. Connolly's public house, at 33 Market Square, one of many looted and burned out, was completely destroyed. An impressive four-storey building with the 'Connolly's' sign in large letters above the second-floor windows, it was one of Lisburn's oldest and best-known public houses. It had been in the Connolly family since the 1850s. Now managed by William Henry Connolly and his sister Teresa, the living area above the pub was extensively furnished with antique furniture, as was the billiard room at the rear of the bar. Teresa took a keen interest in fine furniture and had bought furniture in Paris and Brussels. Everything was engulfed by the flames. The Protestant-owned Harvey & Maxwell public house next door survived with minimal damage. The windows of this spirit grocer had its windows, advertising Cadbury's cocoa and chocolate and Dewar's Perth whisky, smashed in the frenzy to burn down Connolly's pub. On the other side of Connolly's, a furniture shop did not have so much as a window broken, but some of the stock suffered smoke damage, as indicated by a later clearance sale. The King's Arms public house in Market Square, while not subject to attack, was nevertheless damaged by flames from the shop next door. A Union Jack flag was later flown from an upstairs window in case there was any misunderstanding about its owners. A number of other Protestant-owned shops that had escaped damage also displayed a Union Jack. A reporter from the *Newsletter* wrote that a visitor to the town could well have imagined that a festival had been taking place as almost every dwelling house and business premises had Union Jacks and other loyalist symbols on display.

When it became obvious on Monday that the rioting was increasing in intensity, a meeting was convened in the afternoon involving the local magistrates and the military to find some way of restoring order. The meeting was also attended by Rev. Swanzy and Canon Carmody. The outcome was to suggest a voluntary curfew and the following notice was drafted for printing and for display throughout the town: 'With a view to the restoration of order in the town all loyal inhabitants are requested to assist the authorities by returning to their homes at 8.00 p.m.' It was signed 'By order of the civil and military authorities.' The notice was displayed but was ignored.

Later that afternoon Canon Carmody organised a meeting of local residents in the schoolroom of the cathedral. The meeting was addressed by Rev. Swanzy and among those present were Rev. Chancellor Banks, E.P. Riddell, J.P. Bradshaw, Ezekiel Bullick, R. Griffith JP, William Ritchie JP, Thomas Walsh, George Duncan and Thomas Clarke. The objective of the meeting was to support the Urban Council in any steps they chose to take to afford assistance to the military and police in the effort to restore peace. The canon referred to the earlier meeting and suggested that those residents who were on the side of order should help the efforts of the military and constabulary. Rev. Swanzy stated that the mother and sister of the late DI Swanzy were anxious that what was going on in Lisburn town should stop. It was agreed at the meeting that a peace patrol would be organised for that evening.

At 7.30 p.m. a specially convened meeting of the Urban Council was held in the town hall. Chaired by Dr St George, the meeting was attended by most of the council, Rev. Swanzy, Rev. Banks and Rev. Carmody, as well as the gas manager, the surveyor and other officials. After much deliberation the following resolution was passed unanimously:

> That the Council as a body go out and patrol the streets and endeavour to enlist the help and assistance of the respectable citizens of the town to endeavour to persuade the crowds to leave the streets and keep in their own houses and thus endeavour to put a stop to the looting and firing of property; this citizens' patrol to get the police and military to accompany them.

The council also decided, with the approval of Mr A.S. Brook, the manager of the gas works, that the gas supply to the town should be cut off night and day for the present.

The peace patrol set out immediately after the meeting had finished. However, despite being supported unanimously by all present, only a couple of dozen were prepared to put on the white armbands and go out to face the crowds. The three clergymen gave good example by going out and appealing to the crowd to disperse and to bring the rioting and looting to an end. They were heckled by the crowd with calls such as 'Give us the scriptures' and 'An eye for an eye'. The UVF members, who had claimed to have calmed things down after the July riot, declined to support the peace patrol.

A Major Harrison, frustrated by the complete lack of co-operation by the public in trying to help defuse the situation later spoke to a reporter from the *Belfast Telegraph*. He asserted 'if civilians had co-operated last evening [Monday] with the military and police and endeavoured to maintain or restore order it would have saved a great deal of property and destruction and the necessity for replacing the same; it would also have induced the raiders to have adopted a more reasonable view.' Instead of agreeing with the major, the council took offence at his comments. Dr George St George, following a hastily convened council meeting on Wednesday, issued a statement rejecting the accuracy of the allegation. He pointed out that the council had organised a peace patrol and that on Monday there were very few military or policemen in the town, the majority of the military being on guard at the convent and the chapel.

In the meantime the mob turned their attention to Bow Street. A small group of members of the peace patrol tried to assist the fire brigade as rioters began with increased fury to burn Catholic-owned premises in Bow Street. The initiative failed almost immediately as they were pushed aside to the sound of breaking glass as shop front windows were smashed. It seemed to matter little to the rioters which other properties were damaged as long as they achieved their objective. A number of families lived above their shops in Bow Street and the objective was not just to destroy their livelihood, but to burn them out of house and home. Devenny's butcher's at 9 Bow Street just opposite the entrance to Graham Gardens was one of the first premises in Bow Street to be targeted. The resulting inferno engulfed not only the butcher's shop, but also Reid's drapery shop next door. The fire consumed the accommodation above the shops and only through the efforts of the fire brigade was Kirkwood's major hardware store at the corner of Bow Street saved. As shop after shop was set on fire families had to flee for their lives.

Among those caught up in the frenzy were Mrs Cherry and her two daughters, a Protestant family that owned a haberdashery and tailoring shop in Bow Street. The shop and their home were completely engulfed in the flames. They had to leave all their personal belongings behind to escape to safety. Peter Tougher, trading as McCann's, had a fruit and vegetable shop in Bow Street. A popular shop in the centre of Bow Street, it had a large plate glass window with two bell-shaped gaslights suspended outside above the window. The large shop window was smashed and the building set on fire. As the fire took hold, burning through the two upper floors and causing the roof to collapse, the glass sign with the McCann name in ornamental script cracked and part of it fell into the street. It was just good luck that the buildings on either side, one the offices of Lockhart solicitors, survived intact.

Commenting on the violence in Lisburn the *Northern Whig* reported: 'A very unfortunate part of the affair is that in several incidences the spread of the flames involved the shops and houses of loyalists in the vicinity of the burning buildings.' The fires spread to Redmond Jefferson's shop, stores and sawmill at 35-37 Bow Street and the flames, feeding on paint and timber, created an inferno and could be seen for miles around. William Wilson's public house at 20 Bow Street also fell victim to the flames and Elizabeth Savage, the owner of a grocer's, hardware and seed merchant store at the corner of Bow Street and Market Place, lost most of her stock. She was fortunate in that the building survived. The remaining public houses in Bow Street, owned by the McKenny family, were looted and burned. McKenny's pub on the corner of Antrim Street and Bow Street and Chapel Hill was also attacked. At one point during the night the conflagration was such that the flames from each side of Bow Street met, making the street completely impassable.

The lawlessness was not confined to the town centre. Across the Union bridge, on the County Down side of town, Rice's public house was looted and burned. The *Belfast Telegraph* later carried a photograph of the burned-out County Down Arms Hotel under the caption, 'This is Lisburn, not Ypres', a reference to the destruction that had taken place in France during the war. The building was completely gutted. The police watched from Union bridge as twenty or thirty men rolled four or five porter barrels away from the pub and towards the bridge. John Lewis from Ballynahinch Road was observed using a sledgehammer to break open a barrel and then distributing the porter to his fellow looters. Looting was a family affair in some cases, with men breaking shop windows and passing the stolen goods out to waiting women and children. There was no attempt at concealment and stolen goods were shared or exchanged with others who might have had too much of a particular commodity. The gutters were filled with empty porter bottles and discarded goods. Shops that survived had remained closed all day and owners were now removing stock to prevent it from being looted. It was a difficult situation for shopkeepers, as they had to persuade drunken men and women that they were not engaged in looting the premises but actually taking their own property to a safe location. Catholic families were also using every kind of vehicle to remove furniture and personal belongings, as the exodus of Catholic families began.

As Tuesday morning dawned the smell of smoke hung over the still smoldering shells of burned-out buildings along what was once one of the main shopping streets in Lisburn. There was an uneasy calm. Tuesday was market day in Lisburn and Market Square was usually crammed with stalls and carts – on this occasion only one trader put in an appearance in the deserted square. Barefoot children – shoes were a luxury in 1920 Lisburn – carefully picked their way through the ruined streets as they examined the devastation. There was an air of foreboding that worse was to come. Exhausted from two days and nights of arson and intimidation, the rioters rested.

And so it was that the funeral of Oswald Ross Swanzy, the second son of the late James Swanzy, a solicitor from Castleblaney, and Elizabeth G. Ross, received scant attention. Only a week earlier, on Sunday 15 August, his mother and sister had helped him celebrate his thirty-ninth birthday – now they were preparing for his funeral. It took place from his home at 31 Railway Street and was a private and relatively low-key event. Mrs Swanzy had placed a dignified death notice in the *Newsletter*. There was no mention of the callous manner in which her only remaining son had been gunned down in the street. The notice simply read:

> SWANZY August 22 1920 in Lisburn. Oswald Ross Swanzy DI Royal Irish Constabulary second and dearly beloved son of late James Swanzy, Castleblaney and Mrs Swanzy, 31 Railway Street, Lisburn. 'The lord gave and the Lord hath taken away. Blessed be the name of the Lord.' Funeral strictly private. No flowers by special request.

Given the impact DI Swanzy's murder had had on the town of Lisburn, it would have been expected that Railway Street would have been lined with mourners. This was not the case. A number of people did gather outside the Orange Hall opposite the house to witness the funeral, but it was a far cry from the scenes at the funeral of Colonel Smyth in Banbridge, a month earlier. The remains were carried the short distance from his home to Lisburn railway station in an oak coffin by uniformed policemen. His body would be transported by train to Dublin for burial. The funeral procession was timed to meet the 10.20 a.m. train from Belfast to Dublin. Royal Irish constables lined the platform to bid farewell to their comrade. The policemen were drawn up in two ranks and as other heads were bowed, they stood to attention and saluted as the train moved out of the station. The grief-stricken Mrs Swanzy, her daughter Irene and Rev. H.B. Swanzy accompanied the coffin to its final resting place in Mount Jerome cemetery at Harold's Cross in Dublin. This was to be the final resting place for many members of the Royal Irish Constabulary.

More Catholic families left their homes. Those who were too ill to leave or had nowhere to go stayed and prayed that their lives might be spared. It is estimated that up to 1,000 Catholics fled Lisburn. On the Sunday after the riots only nine people attended mass – normally there were crowded congregations at the three Sunday masses in St Patrick's church.[11] Those who could afford the rail fare made their way to the railway station with whatever basic necessities they could carry. Many went to Belfast, while others went to Newry and Dundalk. During the day the platforms of Lisburn railway station were lined with families waiting for the next train to take them away from the town. The families leaving Lisburn for Belfast were joined by others when the trains stopped at Hilden, the next station, as Catholic families from the Low Road area of the town clambered on board with what little they could carry. Those who could not afford the fare walked to Belfast and the exodus continued over the next few days. When families making their way to Belfast on foot were attacked at Lambeg, they were forced to turn back and take the mountain road to reach Belfast. Some, who had made it past Lambeg to seek refuge in Dunmurry, the next village, were forced to move on. In Belfast men and women, children in tow, made their way to St Mary's Hall in Bank Street, near the city centre, as the St Vincent de Paul Society had already set up a centre there to deal with Belfast families who had lost their homes. Now families from Lisburn and other towns also made their way to St Mary's Hall to seek refuge. Initially approximately 200 families from Lisburn were provided with accommodation, often in the homes of other Catholics who themselves had suffered from the ongoing sectarian attacks in the city. Contemporary reports told of young and old forced to sleep in the open, with some seeking shelter along the mill wall in Flax Street, off the Crumlin Road.

The number of refugees seeking help and shelter became such a problem that it was necessary to establish the Expelled Workers' Relief Committee. Dealing with those who had either been put out of work and had no income or those who had been put out of their homes and were now homeless, this committee brought together Sinn Féin and Labour representatives. In America in December 1920 wealthy supporters of the new provisional Republican government formed the American Committee for Relief in Ireland (ACRI) to collect funds to help those who had suffered at the hands of the British. There was an element of propaganda associated with the collection of these funds, as it underlined that the suffering inflicted by the British forces was so extensive that international aid was needed. The Irish White Cross Society was later founded in America on 1 February 1921 as an initiative of the then president-in-exile Eamon de Valera, as a relief organisation to disburse funds collected by the ACRI. Its objective was to help refugees and those affected by the Anglo-Irish War on an all-island basis. It distributed over £1,350,00 in aid throughout Ireland in 1921-22, mostly as personal grants and as loans to help with the rebuilding of houses. Many in Lisburn turned to the White Cross for assistance.[12]

As if working to a plan, the rioting flared up again on Tuesday afternoon. The Lisburn fire brigade, under the command of Captain

William Megran, was unable to cope with the number of fires in the town, and the mob would only permit them to deal with fires that threatened Protestant-owned properties. A section of the Belfast fire brigade, from Chichester Street headquarters, was called to assist. They arrived at around 2.30 p.m. and were immediately given the task of dealing with fires in Market Square. But the mob dictated where they could work and frequently cut their hosepipes when they attempted to save Catholic homes or business premises. The military had to fix bayonets at one stage to guard a fire engine. The Belfast fire brigade, coming under frequent attack, realised that it was futile to remain in Lisburn and at 7 p.m. returned to their station in Belfast.

The Railway Hotel, opposite the station, was being used as the headquarters of the military and police officials and even it was not immune to attack. District Inspector Moore was instrumental in saving the hotel from being set on fire, as he spotted a man in the large yard at the rear of the hotel who, when challenged, ran off, leaving a container of petrol behind. It appeared that his intention had been to burn the building.

The Catholic-owned public houses in Smithfield were not so fortunate. John McIlroy's public house at 5 Smithfield, as with other pubs, was looted before being set on fire. Caught up in the anarchy was George Bunting, who was severely injured as he tried to protect his mother's pub as it and James Neeson's adjoining Kentucky Bar came under a sustained attack. Both buildings ended up blackened shells with gaping holes in the slated roofs. Joseph McMullan, 6 Belvoir Terrace, was among those taken from their houses that night to see their furniture dragged into the street and set on fire. Mr McMullan kept lodgers, among them a Constable McCaughey. Catholic homes all across the town were attacked, including Patrick Cullen's home, 69 Grove Street, Miss Catherine McQuillan's, a dressmaker, 27 Ballynahinch Road, Patrick Kearney's, an insurance agent, 9 Old

Hillsborough Road and Patrick McGurnaghan's home, Causeway End.

Having attacked Catholic homes and businesses at the top of the town in Castle Street, Market Square and then in Bow Street the mob turned their attention to Chapel Hill. As the evening wore on crowds started to gather around the ornate Wallace drinking water fountain in the open space in Market Place at the junction of Chapel Hill and the now devastated Bow Street. They faced a line of soldiers who were preventing access to Chapel Hill. Normally the gas lamp on the tall lamppost in the centre of the junction would have been lit but the gas supply in the town had been turned off. At 11 p.m., as darkness descended, looted furniture that was not worth stealing was piled high in Market Place and set alight. The crowd, in possession of ample supplies of looted whiskey and rum, gathered around the bonfire, sang partisan songs and taunted the soldiers who had placed a cordon across Chapel Hill.

The situation was becoming increasingly tense as the crowd, now fortified by alcohol and under the cover of darkness, threw bottles at the soldiers. The armed soldiers held their position. The main targets for the crowd of people milling about Market Place were St Patrick's church and the adjoining St Joseph's Hall on Chapel Hill. Both the church and hall were protected by a strong military force, as was the large Sacred Heart of Mary convent on Castle Street at the other side of the town. There the soldiers were having difficulty in keeping the mob outside the convent at bay as stones and other missiles were fired over their heads at the windows. The officer in charge advised the nuns sheltering inside to evacuate the premises, as it was impossible to guarantee their safety. Transport arrangements were quickly made and while the military held back the mob at the front of the building the nuns made their escape through the garden at the back of the convent. Waiting cars brought the nuns to the tranquil Glens of

Antrim where they sought sanctuary. Eight nuns found refuge in Cushendall, where parish priest Father McCartan, who had known the community well when he had been parish priest in Aghagallon, near Lisburn, made a house available for them. Four others were provided with accommodation by Father George Clenaghan in Glenariffe. The remainder crossed to Liverpool to take refuge in the Sacred Heart convent at Bootle, Liverpool.

After a few weeks some of the nuns ventured back to their convent to help secure the premises, as most of the windows facing Castle Street had been broken. When news of their return spread a crowd assembled outside the convent with a view to finishing the work they had begun. Father James O'Boyle, the newly appointed parish priest of Lisburn, who had previously served in Ballymoney, appeared at the doorway of the convent and berated the crowd for their disgraceful behaviour. He said that they were not true Orangemen and compared them to the principled Orangemen he had known in Ballymoney, threatening to summon those Orangemen to put an end to this intimidation of the defenceless nuns. The crowd eventually backed off. It would be six months before the entire religious community of twenty-eight returned to Lisburn.[13]

Meanwhile on Chapel Hill the military – the Norfolk Regiment – concentrated on protecting the church and parochial hall from being set on fire. The large and by this time drunk crowd was unable to gain access to Chapel Hill past the armed military so, unnoticed by the soldiers, a group broke away from the crowd and made their way up a lane from adjoining Market Street. This lane led to the back of the buildings on Chapel Hill behind the military cordon. Daniel Mooney's public house was carefully selected and set on fire. Known as The Empire Hotel even though it had not been used as a hotel in the past few years, it was a popular public house. It was not long before smoke and flames billowed out of the front windows as fire took hold in the building, the windows cracking with the intense heat. The military, with a blazing bonfire and a howling mob in front of them, and a building on fire behind them, had no option but to pull back and reinforce their comrades protecting the chapel and parochial hall. As they moved back the mob surged forward up Chapel Hill and began attacking Catholic property. An obvious target was Lavery's public house, a short distance on the left from where the military had set up their cordon. Mrs Lavery's, a well-known and popular public house, had served the Lisburn community since the late 1870s and was also a popular boarding house. The mob chose not to attack the bar and it became the only Catholic-owned public house in Lisburn to survive the looting and arson. It still survives today, the exterior unchanged since that time, still displaying the Lavery sign. The reason it escaped is because it was protected by a well-known Protestant in the town. Jack McKee, a local bookmaker, had a room at Mrs Lavery's and was said to be courting one of Mrs Lavery's daughters. He had previously made it known to the crowd that he had a revolver and would shoot the first person who laid a hand on the Lavery property, which was enough to get the crowd to ignore Lavery's and proceed up Chapel Hill.

An attack was launched on the church, but repelled by soldiers. Standing at the top of the steps at the doorway of the church once again was the solitary figure of Fr James O'Boyle. It was said at the time that he threatened to put a curse on the first man to set foot in the building. The mob taunted the soldiers guarding the church and one young man rushed out of the crowd and, to the cheers of the crowd, placed a Union Jack on the railings at the bottom of the steps leading up to the church. The narrow street outside the church was so packed with people that some were forced down Pump Lane directly opposite the church entrance. This lane, which led directly to open countryside, had a row of a couple of dozen or so houses lining one side. On the other side of the lane were fields which ran up to Priest's Lane, a short distance away at the top of Chapel Hill. At the junction of Priest's Lane and Longstone Street was the Catholic presbytery. A group of men armed with hammers and carrying containers of paraffin oil quietly broke away from the crowd and made their way across the fields towards the parochial house.

Frustrated by their inability to attack the church and parochial hall the mob moved on to launch a ferocious attack on all the Catholic-owned property on Chapel Hill. A country postman, who just wanted to make his way home, was caught up in the middle of this mayhem. His way was blocked by the mob and in frustration he took a whistle from his pocket and blew it loudly. The mob, thinking this was a signal for a military charge, immediately scattered. The postman then got on his bicycle and cycled quietly homeward.[14]

The presence of the military did not, however, prevent Catholic public houses from being attacked and reduced to smoking rubble. In addition to Daniel Mooney's public house, Quinn and Downey's public house, on the opposite side of the street just below the chapel, was also destroyed. Originally a thatched cottage bar owned by Mickey Pogue, it had been demolished and replaced with a modern two-storey building by Messers Quinn and Downey. Now that building was totally destroyed, as indeed were the adjoining buildings. Quinn and Downey later rebuilt and the new building was named Hilltown by one of the partners in the business, who originally came from Hilltown in County Down. Lavery's public house survived but the building next to it was destroyed and beyond that 'general dealer' Johnny Maguire's premises were also set on fire and reduced to rubble. William Laverty, who owned a confectionery and greengrocer shop, had his furniture destroyed and the shop looted. Margaret Carrigan's confectionery, cigarettes and religious objects shop was looted and completely burned out. Other premises not burned were wrecked and looted. The mob continued up Chapel Hill and on to Longstone Street, lined on each side with terraced houses.

Here the fury of the mob was focused on the Catholic parochial house. This large residence, set back from Longstone Street and fronted by trees and an impressive circular driveway, was at the corner of Priest's Lane (now Tonagh Avenue) and Longstone Street. The house was unoccupied as the three priests, John Gillen, John Murphy and William Walsh, whose home it was, had left earlier for their own safety. Such was their urgency to escape that they were unable to remove parish records of births, deaths and marriages or personal books and possessions. The group of men, who had taken a circuitous route to avoid any military on Longstone Street who might have been there to protect the parochial house, had already broken into the building. They were now joined by the mob that had made its way up from the chapel, leaving widespread destruction in its wake. They set about ransacking the parochial house and looting its contents.

The funeral of Rev. Mark McCashin, who had died on 3 August and who had been Lisburn's parish priest for thirty years, had taken place a few weeks earlier. Fine table linen, dinner plates and cutlery hired from the Albert Hotel in Belfast for a meal following the funeral service were still in the house and were looted and distributed among the crowd. Books and parish records were taken from the shelves and piled up in the rooms. Paraffin oil was then poured over the books and they were set on fire. It was reported that the rioters danced around in priest's vestments as the building went up in flames. Local folklore suggests that the rioters toyed with the idea of going to the cemetery behind the parochial house and digging up Rev. McCashin's coffin. With flames reaching high into the night sky and lighting up the surrounding area, the mob, unimpeded by police or the military, continued with the orgy of destruction. Because the fire brigade was prevented from accessing the building it was completely gutted. Later the white walls, all that remained of the building, were covered with graffiti which included: 'No Pope or Prists [*sic*] Here', (priests being an addition to a familiar slogan), 'No Home Rule', 'Site for New Orange Hall', 'God Save the King', 'To Hell with the Pope', and 'Hertford Orange Hall'. Crowds of men, women and children were happy to pose in front of the gutted building to have their photographs taken. In one photograph a woman held a Union Jack flag in one hand and a hammer in the other. A young man struck a pose holding a rifle. One young woman who had danced around the burning building wearing priest's vestments was later said to have given birth to a deformed child. This was, in local folklore, seen as retribution by one side of the community and on the other side as a curse placed on her by the clergy.

With the parochial house ablaze, the mob's attention was turned to the homes of Catholics on the other side of the street, although scant thought was given to who or what would suffer as houses were set on fire. Some of the houses had thatched roofs and when a couple of two-storey houses in the centre of a row of houses were attacked and set on fire, the flames soon reached the thatch and spread rapidly to engulf the whole row of houses. Owen Trainor's pub at 34 Longstone Street, which had already been attacked and looted in July, went the way of the other Catholic-owned pubs in the town. At least ten houses were wrecked as the mob moved along Longstone Street. It was only when they reached the end of the town that they stopped.

Lisburn was left in a dreadful state and among those who came to see at first hand the damage caused was Lieutenant Colonel Fred Crawford, the Belfast industrialist who was involved in the importation of guns and ammunition to arm the UVF. His sympathies lay with the unionists who had suffered because fires in Catholic-owned premises had spread to theirs. He wrote:

Lisburn is like a bombarded town in France ... All this is done by Unionists as a protest against these cold blooded murders and the victims are Rebels or their Sympathisers ...We visited the ruins of the Priest's house on Chapel Hill; it was burnt or gutted and the furniture all destroyed ... It has been stated that there are only four or five R.C. families left in Lisburn; others say this is wrong that there are far more. Be that as it may there certainly are practically no shops or places of business left to the R.C.s.[15]

Crawford was so concerned by the destruction of unionist-owned property, not only in Lisburn but in Belfast and other towns too, that he wanted to legitimise the arming of Protestant civilians to defend their lives and property. The logic of this is not altogether clear in the case of Lisburn and other provincial towns, as the destruction of unionist-owned property was entirely the responsibility of unionists themselves. Crawford had already organised and armed about twenty men to protect his factory off the Shankill Road in Belfast from attack. Not only was it a significant chemical factory, but it was also one of the main arms' dumps for illegally imported UVF rifles and ammunition. Using his rank and contacts within the British army, Crawford secured an interview at Dublin Castle with T.J. Smith, the acting Inspector General of the RIC. Smith, incidentally, had also been named in the inquest following the murder of Tomás MacCurtain. In a note about the visit Crawford recorded, 'Went down to see Gen. T.J. Smith to ask the Irish executive to issue automatic pistols to the local lads to defend themselves and their friends from rebel assassins. If Major Ewart had a pistol he could have saved DI Swanzy in Lisburn last Sunday.' Picking up on a point made by the late Colonel Smyth in Listowel, Crawford suggested that if these men were shot they should know that their wives and children would be looked after and they should also be exempt from punishment if arrested. The plan to place a gun in the hand of every male Protestant came a short time later with the introduction A, B and C special constables.

The burnings, destruction and intimidation of the Catholic population in Lisburn were to continue, albeit not on the same scale, for months to come. For the individuals affected the scale of destruction was irrelevant, as the trauma was the same.

Catholic homes in the Low Road area came under attack. Grove Place, off the Low Road, called 'Pope Row' because of the number of Catholic families living there, received particular attention. Most were employed in nearby Barbour's Mill and it was their fellow employees who came to burn them out. Families including Sherry, Costello, Glen, Totten and Hamilton had their furniture forcefully removed from their homes and piled high on the nearby Grove Green and set on fire. Of course anything of particular value, like a sewing machine, was stolen. It was galling for the occupant to know, for years afterwards, that a Protestant neighbour was using their sewing machine and there was nothing they could do about it. The houses were spared because of the danger of the fire spreading to Protestant homes. Behind these houses there were long gardens which were used to grow potatoes and other vegetables to help feed the individual families. Such was the panic when the homes came under attack that mothers hid babies among the broad leaves of the rhubarb patch in the garden as they fled for their lives.[16] Many families, like Mary and James Hamilton and their five children, were evicted. Mary had been a wet spinner in Barbour's Mill and James also worked there as a hoist–man. They were able to survive due to the generosity of the Hendersons, Protestant neighbours, originally from Cork, who provided them with shelter until the physical attacks eased.

The 24 August edition of the *Belfast Telegraph* reported that in Hilden, where a number of Catholic families lived together – apparently making it a largely 'anti-unionist' enclave – Protestants had been ordered to leave their homes, and a contingent of unionists had gone to the area to protect those homes. The story ran again on 26 August, when it was stated that '200 non-unionists' had left the Hilden district and the Low Road area fearing trouble. There is no evidence to support this and it was not reported in the local *Lisburn Standard*, which provided comprehensive coverage of events in Lisburn at that time.

The Catholic families, when they returned to their homes, had to start from scratch to obtain basic furniture such as a table and chairs. They were lucky if they were able to obtain second-hand mattresses to put on the floor. For weeks, and in some cases for months, afterwards Catholic homes could be identified by the hessian bags which were used to cover broken windows and window frames. The mill workers who occupied these small houses were then faced with a further problem. Before they could return to work they were required to sign a certificate which stated 'I ... hereby declare I am not a Sinn Féiner nor have any sympathy with Sinn Féin and do declare I am loyal to King and country'. For some the fact that those who had burned their property were now placing this note in front of them was too much, and they refused to sign. Others, with no income or the prospect of another income, signed and returned to work. Some people who had been forced from Lisburn and had fled in fear to Belfast cautiously travelled from Belfast to return to work. Many, however, left to find work in Scotland and England, never to return.

There were many Protestants, like the Hendersons, who were not willing to join sectarian mob action to evict their Catholic neighbours. It took a brave person, however, to be prepared to take a stand against their co-religionists and protect their Catholic neighbours.

One such case took place in Hill Street. A long, narrow street, lined on each side by old terrace houses, it ran from Market Lane in the town centre to farmland in what was then the end of that part of the town. At the very end of Hill Street were four isolated Catholic families occupying the last four houses in the street. The families who occupied these houses, the two Cairns families, the Murray family and the Duggan family, where particularly vulnerable. Their homes were separate from the row of other houses in the street and, standing on high ground and surrounded by open fields, they would be easy to attack and set on fire without any danger of the fire spreading to Protestant-owned property. The blaze would be seen all over Lisburn and across the River Lagan to the County Down side of the town. As a mob made its way up the steep incline, intent on burning these houses, a lone Protestant walked out of his house and stood in the middle of the street armed with a shotgun. He threatened to shoot the first man who tried to go past him and was adamant that the Catholic families were not going to be attacked. The crowd, which had previously had *carte blanche* to evict Catholic families and burn their property, largely unhindered by the police or military – and had certainly never been threatened with being shot – backed down and retreated to seek easier targets. If the police and military had received orders to act in a similar manner as this lone man then much of the destruction in Lisburn might not have taken place. There were a number of cases where Protestants protected their Catholic neighbours. They were later called 'Rotten Prods' by their co-religionists.

At the bottom of Hill Street in Barnsley's Row, in The Hollow lived the McConnell family. William McConnell had witnessed the start of the burnings, and as the systematic destruction spread he, along with other Catholic families in the area, feared for his and his family's lives. At the height of the rioting Mr and Mrs McConnell left their home every evening with their children Hugh, William, Elenore, Henrietta, Jackie and Veronica. They made their way across the fields to hide among the bramble and blackberry bushes that lined the banks of the River Lagan. They spent the night there, returning early the following morning. They were not the only Catholic family sleeping in the open along the Lagan. When their Protestant neighbours learned what was happening each night they banded together and promised that no harm would come to the family. (This neighbourly act of kindness would be remembered two generations later when a member of the McConnell family spoke to me.)

At the height of the destruction, groups of armed men set up road blocks around Lisburn, stopping cars and questioning occupants. Cars were searched and if they were found to be carrying a spare can of petrol it was confiscated to be used later in arson attacks.

Maria Ferris, 3 Sandymount Terrace, Longstone Street, thought she had escaped the burnings. However, on 28 August, six days after the rioting had started, when she was out of her house, it was attacked and set on fire. She was left homeless, as was her lodger, local schoolteacher Mr Fitzsimons.

On market day, a month later on 28 September, a local woman who ran a small dealer's shop got into a dispute with some countrywomen and called them 'Carson's pigs'. She was immediately attacked by the other women, who pelted her with stones, rubbish and onions. The attack continued until the police arrived. They put up the shutters on the shop and dispersed the crowd that had gathered. Between 8 and 9 p.m. that evening, however, crowds began to gather in Market Street and it was obvious that trouble was brewing. The town's fire bell was sounded to summon the fire brigade and the special constables. The first incident was the smashing of the window of a barber's shop on Railway Street. The crowd was moved on by the police and it was later, some distance away, that two houses in Church Street were broken into and wrecked. Further violence took place even further away at Quay Street, where four houses were wrecked. At 10.45 p.m. in nearby Gregg Street, where many of the houses had thatched roofs, a further three houses were broken into and the furniture thrown into the street and burned. It was pure luck that the whole street did not go up in flames, given that a spark could easily have been carried by the wind to one of the roofs. The fire brigade succeeded in putting out the fires and the crowd, seemingly satisfied with their night's work, started to drift off. As a parting shot, however, the shed and stables of a coal dealer were set ablaze. When the fire brigade returned to the scene the commotion caused the crowd to regroup. As the fire took hold and threatened other premises, the situation seemed to be getting out of control and the fire bell was again sounded to call up more special constables. When they arrived a baton charge was ordered to clear the area. This caused a stampede towards Sloan Street and the mob made its way to the centre of the town. The police there funnelled them down into the still devastated Bow Street and kept a watchful eye on them until they dispersed in the early hours of the morning.

The following night a large crowd again gathered in Market Square and the special constables had to be called out once more. They usually came on duty at 9 p.m., but at 7 p.m. the size of the crowd was such that they were called out early. The crowd moved into Railway Street intent on finishing the job they had started the previous night and preventing its owner from resuming his livelihood as a barber. An attempt was made to loot the shop and steal and burn his equipment. A police baton charge cleared the street.

The crowd continued to hang about Market Square, watching the police manning a traffic checkpoint. A car had been stopped and the driver produced his police permit and licence, and was allowed to proceed. However, as it accelerated away one of the occupants leaned over the side of the car and shouted 'Up the Rebels, Good bye-e!' This was like a red rag to a bull and the crowd reacted in a predictable fashion. Fortunately the police motor car was parked nearby and a number of special constables piled into it and gave chase. The car had however been stopped by another patrol on Longstone Street.

The occupants, two young men and two girls, were arrested and brought to Smithfield police station, at the corner of Barrack Street and Smithfield Street. It turned out that these young Protestants had been returning to Lurgan from an opera and, in high spirits, had shouted 'Up the Rebels' as a joke. As they were personally known to some of the police constables no charge was made and they were allowed to proceed home. The crowd, in an angry mood, had in the meantime gathered outside the police station and had to be persuaded to let them go unmolested. To ensure a safe exit from the town they were accompanied by a number of constables. The young people did not realise just how fortunate they had been. If the crowd had reached them before the police, the outcome could have been very different. They were also fortunate that they had been stopped by another police patrol. A few days earlier the police had fired on a taxi that had failed to stop at a checkpoint and the shot narrowly missed the driver and his two passengers.

The following night heavy rain discouraged crowds from gathering again. It was during this week that the convent was again attacked and rooms ransacked. A compensation claim made later revealed that damage included the following: glass in windows, window frames, sashes and woodwork, doors, piano, harmonium, school books, six presses containing kindergarten accessories, weights and scales, a clock, two valuable ornaments, and other goods and chattels in the schoolroom. A permanent military post was established outside the convent to guard the building.

While the frenzy of violence in Lisburn town tapered off, the campaign of attacks on Catholic homes continued in rural areas. The home of John Griffen, a farm labourer from Clogher, was destroyed on 3 September. He had previously fled the house along with his wife and six children, fearing for their lives. Although he was only earning £1 per week he had been provided with food and his accommodation was rent-free. He could not find accommodation elsewhere and had no option but to return to the house. When he returned however, he found that there was nothing left in the house. All of the family's possessions had been stolen or destroyed. He later lodged a compensation claim, but this was dismissed by the judge who claimed that no riots had taken place on 3 September. He refused to adjourn the case to allow the police to give evidence that the house had in fact been attacked. Perversely the judge made an award of £10 to Patrick Doyle of Edentucollo, Hillsborough in respect of damage to his house on 2 September.

15

No Regrets

The RIC Inspector General's confidential report for August 1920 included a summary of events in Lisburn:

> About 1.00 p.m. on 22 August D.I. Swanzy was shot dead in the public street of Lisburn as he was returning from church. This officer had been transferred from Cork for his own safety as Sinn Féin pretended to suspect him of conniving at the murder of the Lord Mayor of Cork. As soon as news of Mr Swanzy's murder got out serious rioting broke out. The houses of all Sinn Féiners and those suspected of being in sympathy with the movement were attacked, some burned to the ground. This developed into an attack on Roman Catholic and Nationalists generally.

After three days and nights of one-sided violence, in which at least one life was lost in Lisburn, over 1,000 Catholics had to flee from their homes and leave behind their businesses. The damage was assessed as being in excess of £810,000, but the report paints a fairly superficial picture of what actually occurred. Despite the presence of police on the streets observing the destruction, only seven men were arrested and charged with rioting. Out of the thousands, according to police reports, who went on the rampage through Lisburn, a total of seven individuals were to be held responsible for damage caused in the town. Of these seven men, five were convicted and sentenced to three months' imprisonment with hard labour. They immediately lodged an appeal and were released on bail pending a further court hearing in January. Finally in April a decision on the appeals from Henry Magee, Millbrook Road; James Lewis, Ballynahinch Road;

William Hooks, Derriaghy; Arthur Kidd, Hill Street and George Lowry, Church Street was made. Their sentences were to be recorded and they were set free.

It has been claimed that the riots in Lisburn in July and August 1920 were spontaneous outbursts in response to the brutal murders of Colonel Smyth and DI Swanzy. This may have been true, to a certain extent, in Banbridge, as feelings ran high following the massive turnout for Colonel Smyth's funeral. The funeral itself was a high-profile affair, with the attendance of key figures from the military and the RIC, and was a spectacle never before witnessed by the people of Banbridge. There is evidence however that the UVF took an active part in orchestrating the violence in the town. The unprecedented violence which followed in Belfast, Dromore and Lisburn and other towns cannot be said to have been spontaneous. There is ample evidence that anti-Catholic attitudes had been encouraged for political ends and in July, when anti-Catholic feeling is at its highest with the Orange Order demonstrations, it was going to take little to unleash the pent-up sectarianism. It must be remembered that in October, when Colonel Smyth's brother Osbert was murdered in Dublin, and when his funeral took place to the same Banbridge cemetery, there were no calls for reprisals. Osbert, like his brother, had also been a decorated war hero and had died in action, but his death passed almost unnoticed by those who had claimed the death of his brother as the justification for evicting Catholics from work and home, and for looting and burning the same.

In Lisburn the murder of DI Swanzy provided the rationale for the UVF in the town to implement a plan to drive the Catholic population out of Lisburn. The action against Catholic property in July had met with little resistance from the police and indeed Swanzy's reluctance to prosecute anyone for the July riots encouraged the more serious attacks in August.

The murders of Smyth and Swanzy were used to justify one of the worst outbreaks of sectarian violence in the north of Ireland, principally in Belfast. The violence continued from 1920 to 1922 and brought Protestants and Catholics into a murderous conflict that resulted in the deaths of 455 and left over 2,000 injured.

It is perhaps interesting to note that among the few who publicly expressed unconditional sorrow at the death and destruction in Lisburn were Elizabeth and Irene Swanzy, the mother and sister of DI Swanzy. In a notice placed in the *Lisburn Standard* on 6 August, deploring the violence, they said that they 'were grieved beyond measure at the destruction and loss which has befallen Lisburn' and 'were sorry that any person should have suffered any sorrow or loss on account of him'.

Mrs Swanzy and her daughter decided that they could no longer stay in Lisburn and moved to Dublin. In February 1921 Mrs Swanzy had a memorial to her son erected in Lisburn Cathedral. A simple and dignified brass plaque paid tribute not only to her son but to all his comrades who had been killed in the service of their country. Below the crest of the Royal Irish Constabulary it reads:

In proud and ever loving memory of
Oswald Ross Swanzy DI Royal Irish Constabulary
Who gave his life in Lisburn Sunday 22nd August 1920
And of all his gallant comrades who like him have been killed in the
unfaltering discharge of their duty and in the service of their country.
'Be thou faithful unto death and I will give thee a crown of life'
Erected by his mother and Irene his sister.

A broken-hearted Mrs Swanzy died in Dublin the following year, in 1922. Later Irene, single and with a substantial inheritance, went on a world tour, eventually marrying and settling in the Fiji Islands. She married Mr Wise, a Civil Engineer and Director of Public Works in Fiji and lived at Princes Road, Tamavua, Suva, Fiji.[1] However, she never forgot her brother and his murder had a profound effect on her. Every year on the anniversary of his death she had a memoriam notice inserted in the *Newsletter* and each year she carefully considered a different biblical quotation to be included in the notice. On 21 August each year, for over six decades, until her own death, the *Newsletter*'s memoriam section included the notice:

> **Roll of Honour**
> Swanzy – In proud and ever-present memory of my brother, Oswald Ross Swanzy, DI, Royal Irish Constabulary, killed in Lisburn, Sunday, August 22, 1920, and to the splendid and imperishable memory of all his gallant Comrades, Officers and Men of the Royal Irish Constabulary, killed in the faithful performance of their duty, 1919–1922.

Canon Carmody, writing in the September issue of the *Lisburn Cathedral Parish Magazine* about the August riots, acknowledged (without actually saying so directly) that innocent Catholics had suffered. He could not, however, resist partly justifying the arson and destruction of property by incorrectly, and without any evidence, implicating local Catholics in the murder of Swanzy. He studiously ignored the plight of the large number of Catholic families forced to leave the town and wrote:

> It is also known that such a crime could not have been committed without aid from some local source, in sympathy with the murderers. These things led unfortunately to reprisals. Every suspected person had his house raided and there began a series of burnings and lootings that continued for two or three days and nights. The result is that an immense amount of property had been destroyed. For some time the appearance of the town, with the glare of the burnings and the immense clouds of smoke, reminded one of the pictures of the bombarded town in Flanders that we saw in the illustrated papers a few years ago. It was very distressing to see it all and to know that the property destroyed was not the property of Sinn Féiners but mostly of people who were loyal.

He went on to add that the reprisals were 'so utterly anti-Christian and so inexcusably wrong'. He referred to the events as a nightmare and said that he found it difficult to get things into their true perspective. His somewhat confused thinking led him to write:

> ... but now the murderers know that they can not come into a town like Lisburn and frighten the people into silence and inaction. They have seen that there is a public spirit which may be roused to do dangerous things – and that will surely be a wholesome lesson for those who think they can carry out their ends by acts of crime and violence.

Sir Edward Carson was not one to show much sympathy for the Catholics who had suffered as a result of the riots either. One of the Catholic victims of the Belfast riots, Michael Cunningham, wrote from County Durham to Joseph Devlin MP, saying that he and his two sons had served through the war – 'all have suffered from wounds and gas' – and had been driven from their home in Belfast 'to look for a living among strangers'. He went on to say that hundreds of other ex-servicemen had been expelled for no other reason than their Catholic faith. Devlin passed the letter on to the Prime Minister, who asked Carson to reply. Carson's reply read:

> Of course such a case, is most discreditable, if true, to Belfast. I have no doubt in the early outbreak in the shipyards and elsewhere after the murders of Smythe [sic] and Swanzy, there were cases which were dealt with without any discrimination, but I believe myself that the Special Constables, if properly selected, will go far to prevent similar cases occurring and I need hardly say that I will have this particular case investigated.[2]

16

Birth of the Ulster Special Constabulary

Lisburn Urban Council certainly did not consider expressing condolences to the family of the unfortunate individual burned beyond recognition in Donaghy's factory, or regret that so many Catholics had suffered the loss of homes and business and had to flee for their lives. On the afternoon of Saturday, 28 August, the week in which the riots had taken place, Dr St George convened a meeting in the assembly rooms to 'consider the advisability of enrolling special constables for the preservation of the peace and the protection of property in the urban district'. Dr St George and the other members of Lisburn Urban Council realised that there had been total anarchy in the town during the week and it appeared that the street violence would continue into the next week. They could not depend on the British government to provide the necessary police or military to bring the situation under control. The RIC was stretched to its limits in Belfast, dealing with some of the worst sectarian rioting ever seen in the city. It was also under severe pressure in the south-west of Ireland, where mass resignations and the regular murders of officers had reduced its effectiveness as a credible police force. It had only recently been bolstered by the recruitment of former soldiers, the Black and Tans, from England and Scotland.

The initial intake of the Black and Tans had been posted to the provinces of Munster and Connaught and it was some time before they moved north to Ulster to support the police there. Likewise it would have been difficult to make a case to the British government to provide extra soldiers to control rampaging loyalists who professed to be British and were not under attack. In other parts of northern Ireland, where there were attacks by the IRA on police barracks and courthouses, vigilante groups were formed by the Protestant community. These vigilantes, using their own weapons or old UVF weapons, mounted patrols to check the movement of strangers in their districts. Captain Sir Basil Brooke in County Fermanagh had been at the forefront in organising vigilantes 'as a support for the police' and had made a case to the authorities in Dublin to have an official special constabulary appointed. His proposal was rejected out of hand, as the government had no desire to see yet another armed group over which it would have little control. While support for the police in helping to maintain law and order was welcomed, the government made it clear that it would not, in any circumstances, condone the arming of members of the public who purported to provide such support.

However on 23 July 1920, at a conference in London involving British ministers and officials from the Irish administration in Dublin, this attitude weakened. In many ways this was a crisis meeting, as conditions in Ireland were deteriorating and most of the meeting was taken up with discussions on whether to seek a truce with Sinn Féin, or to introduce more draconian measures to defeat the IRA and break Sinn Féin. The doves at the conference supported a truce, taking the line that further repression would create a situation like that which followed the executions of the leaders of the 1916 Rising, merely turning more and more people against the British in Ireland. The hawks, such as General Tudor and Sir James Craig, who was present as Parliamentary Secretary to the Admiralty, and Winston Churchill, the Secretary of State for War, took the view that they could only succeed if a policy of repression was introduced.

They were in many ways endorsing the policy that had been

articulated by the late Colonel Smyth in Listowel barracks. It was Churchill who suggested that consideration should be given to providing Protestants in the six counties with arms and charging them with keeping law and order in their own areas, so that police and military resources could be redeployed to the south of Ireland. Sir John Anderson, Joint Under Secretary at Dublin Castle, thought such a policy would be disastrous, as it would alienate moderate nationalists and make it easier for the IRA to recruit more members. In his opinion such action could lead to civil war. The hard-line General Tudor supported the line being taken by his close friend Churchill and pressed home the view that law and order in the north of Ireland could only be maintained if groups of loyal citizens, such as those organised by Sir Basil Brooke, were officially recognised. In a carefully orchestrated debate, Sir James Craig spoke to say that he saw a certain merit in the proposal put forward by Churchill and that these individuals could become special constables, properly sworn in and taking the oath of allegiance. Prime Minister Lloyd George, who was chairing the conference, was persuaded by the prospect of special constables, resulting in the release and redeployment of police and soldiers.

The Irish problem was not the Prime Minister's only problem at that time and he was willing to consider any solution that would give him some breathing space. He was facing similar problems in India, where Mahatma Gandhi was leading a revolt against British rule in India, and in Egypt there was also a growing demand for independence. There was also an upsurge of nationalism in Iraq following the British invasion a few years earlier, and he was still dealing with the aftermath of the third Anglo-Afghan War. There was considerable pressure not only on Britain's military resources, but also on the Treasury funding Britain's military operations abroad and in Ireland. Keen to grasp at any straw, he decided that the matter was worthy of further consideration. He may have chosen to ignore the fact that Tudor, Churchill and Craig had a different agenda – the creation of a private army.

It was against this background that Dr St George sat down to chair the meeting of Lisburn Urban Council that Saturday in August. He explained that he had called the meeting because of the brutal murder that had taken place in their law-abiding town. He did not condemn the violence that had taken place but merely thought it had been taken too far, so it would appear that he was prepared to tolerate an acceptable level of violence against the Catholic citizens of the town. District Inspector Moore had been asked to attend the meeting and to explain the legislation relating to the recruitment of special constables. He went on to say that the town would be divided into districts and that the constables would select their own officers. To applause from his audience he added that he was sure that when they took the oath they would do their duty, as many had done in the war, to king and country. It would appear that he anticipated ex-military personnel joining the ranks of a special constabulary. Captain Woods, commander of the UVF in Lisburn, who had narrowly missed being shot as the killers of DI Swanzy made their getaway – again to applause – moved that they should now get on with the job of appointing special constables. He was seconded by Mr H. Mulholland, a solicitor, who requested that the proposal be acted on immediately. It was agreed that a further meeting be held the following Monday for enrolment purposes.

The adjourned public meeting was again held in the assembly rooms under the chairmanship of Dr St George. The large hall was filled to capacity. It had been arranged that County Inspector R.D. Morrison would be appointed to command the special constables in Lisburn. A solicitor by the name of Joseph Allen, in recommending Morrison, said that 'a general desire had been expressed that Mr

Morrison should be become honorary commandant of the Lisburn special constables'. The motion was seconded by William Ritchie, JP. Mr Morrison accepted the role and as the *Lisburn Standard* reported, 'a considerable number of the steadiest and most responsible citizens were sworn in as Special Constables'. This was the birth in Lisburn of what would later be known as the Ulster Special Constabulary and it is interesting to note that, as in east Belfast, it was brought into being not to control the activities of the IRA but to attempt to control fellow loyalists. The rationale for recruiting special constables – to control the street violence in Lisburn – was something of a red herring. The recruitment of a relatively small number of special constables working with the police and army should have been sufficient, but Dr St George and his colleagues on the Urban District Council were tuned in to the thinking and plans of Carson and Craig. By appointing special constables at this time Dr St George, his colleagues and the police had acted without the approval of parliament, although legislation was in place to allow for the recruitment of special constables. In any event, approval was to be granted a week or so later. Recruitment posters for special constables were immediately printed and pasted on walls and buildings. Many photographs of buildings burned out after the August riots feature the white recruitment posters pasted on their walls. In the event, 800 special constables were sworn in just in the Lisburn area.

In the aftermath of the riots the usual round of official enquiries commenced and reporting on the rioting, looting and arson in Lisburn did not fall to Dublin Castle, but to a newly appointed official in Belfast. The Chief Secretary for Ireland, Sir Hamar Greenwood, had established a secretariat in Belfast to help manage affairs in the north of Ireland. This had been agreed following a meeting of ministers in London on 2 September 1920, which was attended by Sir James Craig. At this meeting Craig said that the loyal population was losing faith in the government protecting them and was threatening a recourse to arms. He therefore predicted a civil war. Taking up the argument he presented at the July conference, he proposed that a 2,000-strong special constabulary, recruited from the loyal population, be created and an Under Secretary appointed in Belfast, with the military and police under his authority. He also suggested that the armed UVF could come to the assistance of the military in the event of a major disturbance.

The decision to approve the formation of a special constabulary and to appoint an Under Secretary in Belfast was ratified by the Prime Minister on 8 September 1920, although this was not made public until 22 October 1920. In reaching this decision Lloyd George chose to ignore the fact that a number of the special constables appointed by Lisburn Urban Council had been charged with rioting and looting in the town and further charges were pending in relation to rioting by other special constables. He also ignored the fact that three Belfast special constables – Redmond's Volunteers – wearing armbands and carrying batons, were caught robbing a Catholic-owned public house in the Ballymacarrett area of Belfast. He further overlooked the fact that members of the Dromore UVF supervised the expulsion of Catholic families from Dromore and that many UVF units joined the new special constabulary with their UVF commanders appointed to senior positions within the special constabulary, as was the case in Lisburn.[1]

The decision to appoint an Under Secretary in Belfast was another coup for Craig, reducing the influence of Dublin Castle in the affairs of the north of Ireland. Craig had been concerned for some time that James MacMahon, a Belfast-born Catholic educated by the Christian Brothers in Armagh, who worked alongside Sir John Anderson as Joint Under Secretary in Dublin Castle, might be influencing policy in relation to the north of Ireland. His worst fears about James MacMahon were he felt justified following the arrest of Kevin Barry, an eighteen-year-old medical student who was an active member of the IRA. Barry was part of an IRA unit that launched an attack on British soldiers collecting bread supplies from Monk's bakery in Upper Church Street, Dublin in September. Three soldiers were killed and two wounded, but as the IRA unit withdrew young Barry was left behind, struggling to free his jammed .38 Mauser automatic pistol. He was discovered hiding under the soldiers' lorry and arrested. He was tried by court-martial on 20 October and sentenced to death by hanging.[2] James MacMahon and Sir James Henry Musson Campbell, the Lord Chancellor, were the only establishment voices who appealed for clemency.[3] Kevin Barry was executed on 1 November 1920. Craig would have been made aware of MacMahon's sympathy for this young IRA man and this would have reinforced his decision to sideline, wherever possible, Dublin Castle officials.

By setting up this new department in Belfast and securing the appointment of an official who met with his approval, Craig effectively reduced MacMahon's and indeed Dublin Castle's scope to interfere with his plans. Although the department would report to Dublin Castle, he ensured that it was granted a great degree of autonomy. Known as the Chief Secretary's Belfast branch, this new secretariat was headed by Sir Ernest Clarke, CBE. Clarke had entered the Whitehall civil service in 1882 and made steady progress through the ranks. In 1904 he was seconded to the Cape Government and spent a year in South Africa. On his return he was placed in charge of the first district (City of London) of the inland revenue income tax service. He was employed by inland revenue for the next thirty-five years, rising to the rank of Deputy Chief Inspector and Assistant Secretary to the Board of Inland Revenue. In 1919 he was appointed Secretary to the Royal Commission on Income Tax and the following year he was knighted on the recommendation of the commission's Lord Colwyn.

Clarke had previously worked alongside Sir John Anderson, who had been a former chairman of the board of inland revenue before being posted to Dublin Castle. Anderson had recognised Clarke's skills in administration and his ability to deal effectively with complex legal matters. In 1920 Anderson offered Clarke a promotion and a complete change of career by asking him to head up the chief secretary's office in Belfast. Along with other civil servants Clarke, with the rank of Assistant Under Secretary for Ireland, set up office on 16 September in the prestigious Scottish Provident Building across from Belfast city hall on Donegall Square West. (This group later formed the nucleus of the Northern Ireland Civil Service.)

One of his first tasks was to attempt to get the thousands of Catholic workers who had been forced from their places of employment by fellow workers back to work. He met with some initial success in persuading Protestant employees to abandon the requirement that Catholic workers sign a document stating that they did not support Sinn Féin before they could resume work. However an upsurge in IRA activity in Belfast at that time, with attacks on the RIC, resulted in a hardening of attitudes and religious discrimination in employment continued. It was ironic that Clarke himself would become involved in religious discrimination whilst holding this office.

The change from inland revenue to the chief secretary's office was not without its difficulties for Sir Ernest. From a department with a long tradition and well-established procedures he found himself, in many respects, starting from scratch. One of his early administrative duties was to recruit staff for his new office, a procedure on which he had been briefed and one which was to introduce him to the endemic sectarianism of Belfast.

Religious discrimination in employment had been a feature of life in this part of Ireland for many years and received an official seal of approval by Sir Ernest when he chaired the panel to recruit staff. An article relating to the selection panel conducted by Sir Ernest appeared in the *Freeman's Journal* on 1 October. He had conducted interviews with two males and two females and found the two males suitable and offered them a position. As they were leaving he called them back and said, 'Pardon me, I omitted to ask what religion you were?' The individuals replied that they were Catholics and later reported that Sir Ernest had replied, 'I am sorry but my instructions are not to appoint officials of your creed. As a civil servant who has worked with all creeds in different parts of the Empire I personally regret this. My instructions however are clear and explicit.' It would appear that his new local political masters were laying the ground rules. He would, of course, have been aware that government departments including Dublin Castle had been infiltrated by Sinn Féin sympathisers, mainly from the Catholic population, and did not wish to see this repeated in his Belfast office.

On the day the article appeared, he wrote to Sir John Anderson in Dublin Castle, disputing the version of events printed in the newspaper. He confirmed that he had asked a man about his religion, but added that in any case he would not have engaged him. He continued, 'as far as possible I am trying to fill my office with Englishmen and Scotchmen [*sic*] but where I am necessarily compelled to take people from the locality (or men with technical knowledge from Dublin). Broadly speaking I must take Protestants or I cannot succeed here.'

This matter continued to cause Sir Ernest concern and he again wrote to Anderson on 4 October, claiming that he did not know the religion of his staff but that he had ascertained, accidentally, that the watchman – a retired police sergeant – was Roman Catholic. He went on to say, 'sectarian differences are at the root of all political differences and administrative difficulties here'. Referring to three members of the Dublin chief secretary's staff, who had been accused of being associated with Sinn Féin he went on to say, 'in these circumstances I believe it would be fatal to any chance of my success if I had in a responsible position in my office a Roman Catholic. I need not say that I deplore that this should be so.' He added that he was prepared to employ English or Scotch [sic] civil servants who might have a chance of being regarded as impartial.

Sir Ernest was very aware of the personal risks he faced in the volatile political climate in Belfast in 1920. In a letter on 9 October to General Henry Tudor, setting out his thoughts on creating and arming a new police force which he felt should be modelled on General Tudor's mobile Auxiliary organisation, he added a postscript, 'PS You mentioned a particular make of revolver, I think it was a .38 as being very good. Could you spare me one and enough ammunition not only to carry when I am going about but to enable me to have a little practice (my sole amusement at present).' In a handwritten reply dated 13 October Tudor said that he was getting .38 Webleys for pocket use by the police. He said that he had some spare ones and had ordered 300 more. He went on to say that he hoped to come to Belfast after attending Smyth's funeral in Banbridge. (For details of the murder of Major Smyth, brother of Colonel Smyth, see Chapter 21.) Sir Ernest's own firearm was to be delivered personally by General Tudor.

17

The Lisburn Mutiny

One of Sir Ernest Clarke's early duties was to report back to the government on events in the north of Ireland, and this included the Lisburn riots. The situation in Lisburn in October was still a cause for concern.

On 14 October 1920, when the six previously mentioned men were charged at the local petty sessions with riot, and five were sentenced to imprisonment (one case was adjourned because an important witness was ill), trouble again flared in Lisburn. That night thousands gathered in Market Square to protest the verdict of the court. This was despite the fact that no one had actually been committed to prison, they had all been released on bail. The crowd was in an angry mood and further violence in Lisburn seemed imminent.

As the crowd milled about the square the by now usual parade of special constables for duty that night was taking place in the assembly rooms under the command of Mr Morrison. A large number of the men who had reported for duty also expressed dissatisfaction with the court's decision. It may seem strange that police constables were prepared to protest about individuals who had pleaded guilty to a crime and were properly sentenced in court. The reason will however become clear later.

The mood among these special constables was such that they handed in their resignations to their commandant to express their outrage at the judge's decision. Morrison was now faced with the prospect of these men going out into the Square and joining the crowd and the prospect of a repeat of the August riots loomed large. Some of what were described as 'leading residents' were also present in the assembly rooms and they were also concerned by the mood both inside and outside the room. They urged Morrison to try to control the situation. Addressing the crowded room he told them that, as special constables, they had to have confidence in him and that he in turn had to be able to trust them, which he could not do if they acted in this way. He told them that their action would lead to the break-up of the special constables' organisation and irreversible damage. In those circumstances he could not help them but if they restrained themselves and left matters in his hands, he would place the views of those protesting before the proper authorities. By using, as he said later, every ounce of influence and authority, they agreed to take no further action. However the promise not to proceed with the mass resignations was conditional on no further action being taken in about twenty other rioting cases which were pending, in addition to those already prosecuted. Morrison agreed to make representations on their behalf. The atmosphere cleared almost immediately and those who had resigned asked to be reinstated. Word went out into the Square that a deal had been done and the crowd started to drift away. The danger of another outbreak of violence had been averted. This incident went unreported in the local unionist *Lisburn Standard*.

On hearing of the special constables' mutiny and the further threat of violence in Lisburn, Sir Ernest Clarke wrote to Morrison on 19 October, asking him to call at his office in Belfast to brief him on the situation.

On 22 October Sir Ernest Clarke attended a meeting with the great and good of Lisburn to be briefed on the events that had taken place, as well as the current situation. On Sunday 24 October Morrison followed up his meeting with Sir Ernest with an eight-page handwritten letter. Having outlined the events which had occurred in the assembly rooms, he went on to inform Sir Ernest of the great danger to the peace of the community should the men convicted be severely punished or if the other prosecutions in connection with the riots were to be proceeded with. He then listed six reasons why no further action should be taken against those convicted or where arrests were pending.[1] Sir Ernest drew heavily on these points when he later prepared his report for the Chief Secretary's office in Dublin. In closing his letter, Morrison said that as peace had been restored chiefly owing to the public-spirited and unselfish action of the special constables, it was expected that matters would be allowed to drop. There was no mention of the mass resignations, the prospect of further violence and the blackmail that had taken place on 14 October. He wrote:

> I appeal to you on behalf of all the leading residents of Lisburn (some of whom you have seen) and on behalf of 25 officers and over 800 men in the Lisburn Corps of Special Constables – which is thoroughly representative of every section of the community – to take such action as you consider the situation demands in view of the facts which I have the honour of bringing to your notice.

This he signed as 'Ex County Inspector and Commander Lisburn Corps of Special Constables'. It is obvious from the note drafted by Sir Ernest Clarke after the meeting that the plight of the Catholic population of Lisburn did not rank highly in their concerns. Instead the main concern was that those found guilty of offences related to the rioting and looting should not be punished, and there was good reason for this, as many of the others identified but not yet arrested were special constables and fellow Orangemen. There was a danger that if these individuals were charged and it was revealed that they were special constables and/or members of the UVF, it would have serious implications for the Lisburn council officials who had actively been involved in the creation of these bodies. It would also be a serious embarrassment to unionist leaders and the government if it was revealed that a force which had been created to defend against attacks by the IRA had not been under attack but was actively engaged in sectarian onslaughts on Catholic homes and businesses.

Mindful of this, on Monday 25 October, as a follow-up to the meeting and the note from Morrison, Sir Ernest sent a letter to Sir John Anderson at Dublin Castle. On the same day in the House of Commons the nationalist MP Joe Devlin was on his feet asking Chief Secretary Greenwood if the government intended to employ UVF men as special constables and asked him to confirm that 300 special constables in Lisburn had resigned because a number of their colleagues had been convicted of looting Catholic houses. The chief secretary declined to comment on the government employing UVF men as special constables but confirmed that three special constables had been committed for trial in Belfast for looting. Two were on bail and one was in custody. He also confirmed that hundreds of special constables in Lisburn had threatened to resign but did not do so. Sir Ernest's letter is reproduced below:

Dear Anderson,
Lisburn Prosecutions

On Friday evening last I saw at Lisburn, at their request, a deputation of prominent citizens in regard to the prosecutions for rioting and looting on 22nd August – following on the murder of Inspector Swanzy.

Five men have been convicted before the Magistrates on these charges and have been sentenced. They have appealed and at present are on bail waiting the hearing of the cases before the Sessions in January next. I understand that one other man has been summoned but that the proceedings have been adjourned owing to the illness of a witness. There are about thirty other cases which have not yet come before the Magistrates nor have summons been issued. I understand that a report has been made by the County Inspector through the District

Commander in regard to these cases and I believe that an abstention from any further prosecutions has been indicated.

The deputation laid before me for consideration the following points:

That the town of Lisburn had, as a whole, been remarkably free from any crime in the past until the outbreak after Swanzy's murder.

That the outbreak was a spontaneous and sudden expression of feeling – an outlet for the rage of the populace at being unable to punish the actual perpetrators of the murder.

That many thousands of persons took part in the rioting and subsequent looting.

That the men prosecuted and convicted and those summoned were not the leaders and were not distinguishable as being particularly active in rioting and looting. They merely happened to be known by name to the police and as they were present, they were selected for prosecution.

That the previous character of the men was not taken into consideration before deciding to send their names forward.

That a delay of nearly two months took place between the time of the alleged offence and any prosecution.

That many of the men are Special Constables. [The word 'now' was added to the typed manuscript before Special Constables.]

The town of Lisburn is now quiet and I am informed that many of the people who took part in the rioting and looting regret the action taken. There is now a large force of Special Constabulary but when the results of these prosecutions were announced more than half of them tendered their resignations and I am informed by reliable persons that it was only due to the influential inhabitants that a further tumult did not arise in Lisburn.

I do not, of course, know what the purport of the District Commissioner's report and there is obviously only a choice of evils, but I do think that a serious position might arise in Lisburn and might extend to other parts of the Province if the outstanding proceedings against the thirty men were definitely taken. If it is in any way possible, I think it would for the peace of the Province that legal action should be confined to the cases already heard and that no further summons should be issued. I consider the case of these thirty men of the utmost importance as is also the case of the five men already sentenced who have appealed. I understand that the Lord Mayor has written to the Chief Secretary in a similar strain to this.

Yours sincerely

EC

Assistant Under Secretary[2]

The letter sent to Dublin Castle has to be read in conjunction with the draft Sir Ernest had written following the meeting in Lisburn. The sectarian nature and the inaccuracies presented to Sir Ernest – new to the area – by those attending the meeting, come to light. It perhaps also demonstrates a degree of sectarianism at the core of the Chief Secretary's office, as Sir Ernest would not have been so naïve as not to understand the import of his letter, even though it was a toned-down version of the original draft.

In the manuscript note left by Sir Ernest Clarke at the Lisburn deputation he wrote:

> With reference to the disturbances which have lately taken place in Lisburn and it is to the prosecutions which have ensued the following considerations suggest themselves.
>
> Up to the time of the murders of Major [sic] Smyth in Cork and Mr. Swanzy in Lisburn all sections of the community in this town were living amicably together regardless of their political or religious views. Catholics and Protestants worked alongside each other on public works. Catholic shopkeepers made as good a living as their Protestant competitors. (I instance the 17 Catholic public houses which the town has been able to support.) A Catholic doctor had one of the largest practices in the town and Catholics had been co-opted on bodies such as the committee of the Technical Institution and the Board of Governors of the County Infirmary, the members of which, with the exception of co-opted members, were exclusively Protestant.
>
> Further persons of extreme Nationalist and Sinn Féinn [sic] views were tolerated in a community where the very name of Sinn Féinn was abhorrent and the town was remarkably free from crimes of violence or from anything in the nature of organised crime.
>
> When Mr. Swanzy was murdered on a Sunday morning as people were leaving their place of worship the feeling of all right thinking persons (which had already been deeply stirred by the murders of soldiers and police which were daily reported in the press and in particular the murder of Major Smyth) could no longer be restrained and reprisals took place. It must be remembered that for months men had daily read of the most appalling crimes committed – for which no person had been made amenable: the whole system of justice seems to be paralysed and

there is no doubt that people have a real living dread of such occurrences as they read of becoming prevalent in Ulster. Under the circumstances it is not to be wondered that a virile population, deeply stirred by a dreadful crime, should decide on the spot to make abundantly clear that practices which had sympathisers with or at any rate tolerated in other parts of Ireland would not be tolerated in Lisburn and in consequence took stern measures with all whom suspected to be guilty of connivance at the crime or sympathetic with the political party to whom they attributed the crime.

With reference to the looting which subsequently took place it should be noted that large numbers of people did not look upon the act of removing goods from a burning shop as a dishonest act and openly and without concealment took the goods to their own homes. I know personally of respectable country people from the district where I live whose honesty is above all question and would no more think of stealing than I should. I know of people coming into the town with the avowed and deliberate intention of getting what ever they could. The view that they took was that the places were burning and the contents would therefore be destroyed there could be no harm in their taking them.

So far as one can see things in the town have now resumed a fairly normal condition and I think a number of persons who took part in these proceedings now regret having gone as far as they did. Many of them have given assistance to preserve the peace of the town and have joined the Special Constables and the question seems to arise whether any useful purpose can be served by proceeding against persons charged with riot or looting. It would at any rate seem that a careful discrimination should be made between the cases of men of normally good character who acted spontaneously and in the heat of the moment, even if their actions have been prolonged and the case of men of doubtful character who merely made use of the opportunity to exercise their tendencies for looting and disorder.

It is perhaps commonplace to say that most particularly at a time like the present far more harm would be done by the conviction of one person on evidence, the impartiality of which is admitted by everyone than the escape of 10 persons who deserved conviction. The convictions that have already been obtained have been forwarded on the evidence of a Sergeant and a Constable who are Catholics and there is a suspicion, quite uninformed I admit – but still existent – that this evidence is biased. All the more so that in one of the cases there is no doubt that the convicted man gave invaluable assistance from the outset in saving property. The conclusion I have come to is that the ends of justice would be best served by either dropping prosecutions altogether in the case of persons of good character or if it is deemed advised to proceed then upon conviction by putting the accused under a rule of bail.

E. Clarke
Lisburn
Oct 22 1920

In his letter of 25 October to Sir John Anderson he indicated that the seven key points listed were those presented to him by the deputation, and to some extent distanced himself from them. He wrote that Lisburn had as a whole been remarkably free from any crime in the past, until the outbreak after Swanzy's murder. He was aware, as contained in his draft, that there had been serious violence against the Catholic community in Lisburn after the funeral of Colonel Smyth, but he chose not to mention this in his letter.

He claimed that the outbreak was spontaneous, yet there is evidence of men marching in formation to Market Square and there is evidence that armed UVF men were summoned to the town centre by the ringing of the cathedral bell. The fact that the worst of the burnings and looting went on for four days means it can hardly be regarded as a spontaneous reaction. There was a suggestion that as the men arrested and convicted were not necessarily the leaders of the riot – so by inference there must have been leaders directing the violence. In addition to the men convicted he made reference to those not yet charged, and this was the most important aspect of his letter. He wrote that they had been selected for prosecution because they were known to the police. The fact that they were known by name to the police may have been because they had come to their attention before or because they were in fact new colleagues. The background of the men arrested had not been taken into account before they were charged and to confirm the real reason for the deputation, he listed as the final point that 'many of the men are (now) Special Constables'. The 'now' was added as a semantic afterthought but provided a degree of ambiguity as to the status of the men as special constables at the time of the crime.

It is obvious that the deputation had hinted to Sir Ernest that further and more widespread violence was on the cards if action was taken against the thirty men and to emphasise the matter he was advised that more than half the special constabulary had tendered their resignations when it was announced that the thirty men were to be charged. Faced with the prospect of similar destruction in other towns, Sir Ernest chose what he saw as the lesser evil. He suggested to Sir John Anderson that no charges should be made against the thirty men and the appeal by the five already charged should be treated with leniency by the appeal court. In other words the deputation had been successful in their demand that no Protestant or Orangeman suffer for the sectarian attack on their Catholic neighbours in the town of Lisburn.

The draft manuscript left by Sir Ernest indicates the sectarian tone of the meeting when the fact that there were seventeen Catholic-owned public houses in the town and that a Catholic doctor had one of the largest practices in Lisburn was mentioned. In stating that all sections of the community lived together amicably, regardless of religious or political views, he was generally correct. It was only with the approach of the Twelfth of July celebrations that Protestants boycotted Catholic-owned shops. During this period it was a regular occurrence on Saturday evenings for drumming parties to gather outside St Patrick's Catholic church with Orangemen playing Lambeg drums to interrupt evening services in the church. The matter had even been raised in parliament. In more peaceful times, normality would have returned to the town by September.

Perhaps the worst sectarian element in the draft related to the

18

Dundalk Reprisals

The events in Lisburn had a knock-on effect in other towns, but perhaps nowhere more so than in Dundalk, forty miles to the south on the road to Dublin. In an upsurge of violence immediately following reports of the attacks on Catholic families in Lisburn, four policemen on patrol in Jocelyn Street, Dundalk were attacked. Sergeant Clarke and Constables Brennan, Isdell and Witherden were confronted by a group of six or seven men who shouted, 'Hands Up!' and simultaneously discharged revolvers at the RIC officers. Brennan, shot through the heart, died on the spot. The others were wounded, one escaping serious injury as a bullet was deflected by his belt. This triggered sectarian violence in Dundalk: the Sinn Féin hall in Seatown Place and licenced premises owned by Messers McGuill were badly damaged. All the windows in the hall were smashed and the premises looted. McGuill's public house in Bridge Street had its plate glass window smashed and another pub in Market Square had its shutters smashed and its windows broken. James McGuill, owner of the pub in Market Square, had been elected to both the urban and county councils as a Sinn Féin member.

In what was seen by many as a direct reprisal for the burning of Catholic-owned businesses in Lisburn Thomas Craig's large drapery shop at the corner of Market Square in the centre of Dundalk was subjected to an arson attack. A night postman, seeing smoke coming from the building, raised the alarm but the sound of breaking glass had already woken the thirteen shop assistants and servants sleeping

18

Dundalk Reprisals

The events in Lisburn had a knock-on effect in other towns, but perhaps nowhere more so than in Dundalk, forty miles to the south on the road to Dublin. In an upsurge of violence immediately following reports of the attacks on Catholic families in Lisburn, four policemen on patrol in Jocelyn Street, Dundalk were attacked. Sergeant Clarke and Constables Brennan, Isdell and Witherden were confronted by a group of six or seven men who shouted, 'Hands Up!' and simultaneously discharged revolvers at the RIC officers. Brennan, shot through the heart, died on the spot. The others were wounded, one escaping serious injury as a bullet was deflected by his belt. This triggered sectarian violence in Dundalk: the Sinn Féin hall in Seatown Place and licenced premises owned by Messers McGuill were badly damaged. All the windows in the hall were smashed and the premises looted. McGuill's public house in Bridge Street had its plate glass window smashed and another pub in Market Square had its shutters smashed and its windows broken. James McGuill, owner of the pub in Market Square, had been elected to both the urban and county councils as a Sinn Féin member.

In what was seen by many as a direct reprisal for the burning of Catholic-owned businesses in Lisburn Thomas Craig's large drapery shop at the corner of Market Square in the centre of Dundalk was subjected to an arson attack. A night postman, seeing smoke coming from the building, raised the alarm but the sound of breaking glass had already woken the thirteen shop assistants and servants sleeping can spare 400 for Ulster. The question of equipment will be one of the first things that Wickham should settle but uniformity and simplicity is essential so I don't expect to use the Mausers of UVF. I have no doubt that we can get plenty of short service rifles.

This correspondence and the issues facing Sir Ernest perhaps throw some light on the decision to acquiesce to the pleas from council officials in Lisburn, although they had a different agenda. Despite Sir Ernest's experience of the specials in Lisburn he later became a C Special.[4]

What is indisputable is that the events that took place in Lisburn were purely sectarian and the murders of Smyth and Swanzy were not reasons but excuses for what amounted to a pogrom to rid Lisburn of Catholic-owned businesses and Catholic inhabitants.

comment that the convictions already made were as the result of 'evidence provided by a Sergeant and a Constable who are Catholics' with the admission that 'there was a suspicion, quite uninformed I admit – but still existent – that the evidence is biased'.

While Sir Ernest was endeavouring to make sure that the special constables were not prosecuted for engaging in sectarian rioting, looting and burnings in Lisburn he was also planning to increase the strength and firepower of the RIC. This was in anticipation of the force coming directly under his control with the establishment of a parliament in Belfast. (The Government of Ireland Bill, introduced on 25 February 1920, had proposed two Irish parliaments, one of the six north-eastern counties and the other for the remaining twenty-six counties.) Sir Ernest had written to General Tudor on 20 October setting out his view on the number of police officers and the amount of arms that would be required. In this letter it is interesting to observe the close links that the embryonic Northern Ireland government had with the UVF. An option Sir Ernest placed before General Tudor was the arming of the police force with UVF weapons, which were obviously at his disposal. He wrote, 'I understand that there are available in Belfast 24,000 rifles (mixed) (18,00 of which are in the UVF depot). The number of revolvers available is 400-500.'[3]

In his reply on 24 October Tudor informed Sir Ernest that Lt Colonel Wickham, previously chief administration officer on the staff of General Knox in Siberia, was to be appointed as a new divisional commissioner. Wickham assumed responsibility for the special constabulary and was later, in June 1922, appointed as the first inspector general of the newly formed Royal Ulster Constabulary. In response to options presented by Clarke , Tudor wrote:

> As regards the strength of the RIC in Ulster it will probably be better for you to arrange to raise 1,400 instead of 1,000 as though we are getting plenty of recruits from England it will be some time before I

the final point that 'many of the men are (now) Special Constables'. The 'now' was added as a semantic afterthought but provided a degree of ambiguity as to the status of the men as special constables at the time of the crime.

It is obvious that the deputation had hinted to Sir Ernest that further and more widespread violence was on the cards if action was taken against the thirty men and to emphasise the matter he was advised that more than half the special constabulary had tendered their resignations when it was announced that the thirty men were to be charged. Faced with the prospect of similar destruction in other towns, Sir Ernest chose what he saw as the lesser evil. He suggested to Sir John Anderson that no charges should be made against the thirty men and the appeal by the five already charged should be treated with leniency by the appeal court. In other words the deputation had been successful in their demand that no Protestant or Orangeman suffer for the sectarian attack on their Catholic neighbours in the town of Lisburn.

The draft manuscript left by Sir Ernest indicates the sectarian tone of the meeting when the fact that there were seventeen Catholic-owned public houses in the town and that a Catholic doctor had one of the largest practices in Lisburn was mentioned. In stating that all sections of the community lived together amicably, regardless of religious or political views, he was generally correct. It was only with the approach of the Twelfth of July celebrations that Protestants boycotted Catholic-owned shops. During this period it was a regular occurrence on Saturday evenings for drumming parties to gather outside St Patrick's Catholic church with Orangemen playing Lambeg drums to interrupt evening services in the church. The matter had even been raised in parliament. In more peaceful times, normality would have returned to the town by September.

Perhaps the worst sectarian element in the draft related to the in dormitories over the shop. The majority were able to make their way down the smoke-filled stairwell to the street. Elizabeth Wilson from Ballyhooley, Ballynure, County Antrim; Georgina Rice from Ardee and young Alexander Alderdice from Drogheda did not make it and perished in the fire. An attempt had been made to set fire to J.D. Melville's drapery shop on the opposite side of the street but it was spotted in time and the flames were extinguished.

A meeting was organised by Dundalk Urban Council to discuss how the upsurge in sectarian violence in the town could be brought under control. James McGuill informed the meeting that he was aware of a threat to burn down Protestant-owned houses. He said that he had seen a list detailing the houses to be attacked and had produced a gun and threatened those who proposed this attack. Peter Hughes, the chairman of the Urban Council, proposed that the police and military should be withdrawn from the streets saying that if that happened he would guarantee that 'not a mouse would stir on the streets'. This was a common theme with councils in other towns where there were widespread disturbances, but armed RIC officers – who attended the meeting uninvited – despite a protest from the chairman, let it be known that this proposal was not an option.[1] The violence, successfully contained in Dundalk, continued unabated in Lisburn and Belfast.

19

The District Inspector Ferris Incident

It was claimed that the group who murdered Tomás MacCurtain, lord mayor of Cork, was led by two RIC officers – Swanzy and Head Constable John Patrick Ferris, who had served together in Union Quay barracks. While Swanzy was for his safety posted to Lisburn, a quiet loyalist market town, Ferris was promoted to District Inspector and, like Swanzy, he too was posted north. However Ferris, himself a Catholic, now had responsibility for policing the Catholic Falls Road district with its warren of narrow cobblestone streets, home to an increasing number of IRA members. He was based in the Springfield barracks on the Springfield Road in Belfast.

The streets opposite the barracks, the Kashmir Road district, had been the scene of sectarian attacks in the aftermath of the expulsion of Catholic workers from the shipyards and factories in Belfast. In one incident workers going home from the nearby Mackies engineering company on the Springfield Road came under fire. Later that night Catholic homes were attacked, in retaliation, by loyalists from the adjoining Shankill Road district. Many of the residents in the area had to flee their homes, which were then looted and sacked. Stone-throwing escalated to gunfire. The military and RIC used machine guns to bring the situation under control and a number of people were killed by military and RIC fire.

Compared to Swanzy, DI Ferris had drawn the short straw. Not only did he have to deal with increasing sectarian attacks, but the police barracks itself had a bomb thrown at it on 13 April 1921. It was on 23 April that two Auxiliary cadets, Ernest Baran Bolam and John Beets Bales, in Belfast on escort duty from Sligo, were sightseeing in the city centre as they waited for a delayed train back home. They had been spotted earlier in the day by a member of the IRA and were murdered at Fountain Lane near Castle Junction at 9 p.m. As with all such murders it was not long before a reprisal killing took place.

Close to midnight the Duffin family at 64 Clonard Gardens was preparing to go to bed. John Duffin, a teacher in St Paul's school at Cavendish Square, was already in bed when there was a loud knock at the door. His brothers Pat and Dan were still downstairs and called up to John to ask if they should open the door. John replied that they should see who it was knocking so late, even though a curfew was in place. As soon as the door was opened three men entered and shouted, 'Hands Up!' This was immediately followed by several shots. Pat and Dan died at the door of the small kitchen house. Dan had been a First Lieutenant in the local IRA company. John witnessed the murders from the top of the stairs and later described the incident to a *Belfast Telegraph* reporter. He explained to the reporter what had happened and how he and his father had remained in the house with his dead brothers all night because of the curfew. He was afraid to venture out to get a priest to deliver the last rites, as he too was liable to be shot if seen on the streets after midnight. He also mentioned that a dog that had accompanied the men had been trapped inside the house. The long-haired dog howled and scraped at the door, which had been slammed shut as the killers made their escape. The dog was well cared for and obviously not a stray. John assumed that it belonged to the killers and decided not to turn it out on the street.

The following morning District Inspector Ferris, along with other policemen, came to take the bodies to the morgue. This was strongly resisted and the bodies remained in the care of John and his father. District Inspector Ferris took the dog away and there was much speculation in the *Irish News* about the owner. The dog was familiar to at least one person in the crowd that had gathered to prevent the police from removing the bodies from the murder scene. It was said to belong to Sergeant Christopher (Christy) Clarke, a Catholic RIC man stationed along with District Inspector Ferris at Springfield Road barracks.[1] It was recognised as the Springfield Road police station dog. It was claimed that Ferris and Clarke were part of an RIC reprisal team and both were prominent in the offensive against the IRA in that part of Belfast.

A few weeks later District Inspector Ferris, who was the investigating officer for the Duffin murders, had a meeting with parish priest Father Convery in St Paul's presbytery in Cavendish Street, a short distance from the Springfield Road barracks. As he left the meeting that Saturday afternoon he was spotted by three armed IRA men, who then opened fire on him. (Roger McCorley later claimed that he was one of the men who shot Ferris.) Four shots were fired, hitting him in the neck and stomach. He was left for dead as the assassins made their escape across Dunville Park and into the maze of side streets. DI Ferris was, however, still alive and was quickly brought across the road to the Royal Victoria hospital. He survived the assassination attempt.

In reporting the incident the *Irish News* reminded readers that DI Ferris was the officer who had taken charge of the dog left at the Duffin house following the shooting a fortnight earlier. It was implied and certainly believed by the IRA that District Inspector Ferris was involved in the Duffin murders and implicated with the reprisal gangs.

In later life John Duffin seldom spoke of the murder of his two brothers, as he blamed himself for telling his young brothers to open the door during the curfew. He went on to become, in October 1933, the first principal of St Kevin's Boys' Primary School on the

Falls Road. His brothers Dan and Pat were interred in Glenravel cemetery.

While DI Ferris survived his attack, Sergeant Christy Clarke was not so fortunate. He had been targeted by the IRA on a number of occasions and had managed to evade the attempts to kill him. He had a part-time job working in Celtic Park and was involved in greyhound racing (a link with the dog) and had narrowly missed being shot on St James' Road. On 13 March Clarke and Constable Caldwell were making their way back to the barracks following the funeral of two of their colleagues. Two constables, Cullen and O'Connor from Springfield Road barracks, had been shot in the back while on patrol on the Falls Road and had been buried that day in Millfield cemetery. As Clarke and Caldwell walked past Mulholland Terrace on the Falls Road, five or six men who had been hiding in the grounds of nearby St Dominic's convent emerged and opened fire on Clarke. Suspecting, correctly, that Clarke would be wearing a bullet-proof vest, firing was concentrated on his head and lower body. He died instantly. Constable Caldwell returned fire on the gunmen as they escaped down Broadway and may have injured one of them. Danny Rogan, a passer-by, was caught in the crossfire and later died in hospital.[2]

20

Belfast Boycott

One of the repercussions of the sectarian riots in Lisburn, Banbridge and Dromore – and of course Belfast and other towns – along with the expulsion of workers, was the introduction of a boycott of goods from those areas by the Sinn Féin government in Dublin. This was known as the Belfast Boycott and was designed to bring economic pressure to bear in the hope that the government would intervene to alleviate the plight of Catholics in the worst affected towns. It was instigated at the suggestion of Catholic Bishop McCrory. He organised a meeting of influential Sinn Féin members including Seán McEntee, Denis McCullough, Frank Crummey and Father John Hassan. Supported by the Sinn Féin councillors on Belfast Corporation, the Belfast Boycott Committee was formed.[1] Although the boycott was introduced soon after the riots, it was not until February 1921 that a system to monitor the movement of goods from these towns and districts was implemented by the Ministry of Labour. In Dáil Éireann the new Ministry, designed to oust the British Ministry of Labour as arbiter for the settlement of wages in Ireland, referred to the Belfast Boycott as 'a weapon placed in our hands on account of the murders in Belfast of people simply because they refused to sign away their rights to think as they thought best on matters of religion and politics'. The boycott relied to some extent on information on the movement of boycotted goods being passed by workers, carters and railwaymen to Sinn Féin. In the south the IRA attacked lorries and trains that were transporting boycotted goods and while firms were subject to a fine for selling such goods, the IRA had its own methods for enforcing the boycott.

The organisation of the Belfast Boycott involved the country being mapped out into ten areas and an organiser appointed to each. A central office to control operations generally was established in Dublin, and the Belfast office was reorganised. In a report to Dáil Éireann on 17 August 1921 the Minister for Labour informed the Dáil of the work being done to implement the boycott.

The organisers carried out their work splendidly, and effective committees sprang up all over the country, each in direct touch with headquarters and, where possible, in touch with neighbouring committees. Instructions were issued from G.H.Q., I.R.A., for full co-operation between local brigades and the committees. Two clergymen were also appointed to tour the country to secure the support of the priests in the interest of the Boycott.

At present there are close on four hundred Committees in existence, all, with few exceptions, working with great enthusiasm.

Three of our organisers have been arrested, one being subsequently released after a few weeks detention. Their places were filled without delay.

Owing to the heavy work devolving on the Secretaries in Cork, Limerick, and Derry, paid officials were appointed in those places. In Dublin two organisers were employed, and a patrol of volunteers (on the suggestion of the O/C Dublin brigade). Thousands of cases of dealings with Belfast were investigated, and where necessary strong action was taken. Many houses were raided, and Order Books and 'tainted goods' taken away. Several of the leading firms in the city who were proved offending against the boycott were fined up to the extent of £100. The fines in almost every case were promptly paid. By the aid of persons sympathetic a close watch was established on all the railway termini in the city, on the several shipping companies at the Port, and on the carters, so that at present it is practically impossible for Belfast goods to enter or pass through the city directly, undetected. The drapers and other shop assistants have given much valuable assistance in this way.

Early this year a big effort was made by the Belfast merchants to re-open trade. To this end depots were opened in many cross-channel towns, principally Glasgow, Manchester, Liverpool, and London, and the goods sent over here as coming from a purely English firm. Many of the English merchants lent themselves to this. A large amount of this traffic has been detected and stopped. It may be pointed out that this course could only be adopted in the case of surplus stocks which the Pogromists are prepared to dispose of at a loss, as the expense incurred in the roundabout process would militate against ordinary trade prices.

That Belfast is feeling the turn of the screw is evident from the large number of bankruptcies that have occurred and from the knowledge that has come to us that a very big percentage of the surviving firms are only carrying on with the help of mortgages on their premises.

By means of advertisements, this existence of the boycott is being kept forcibly before the public. Hundreds of thousands of leaflets and large posters have been distributed at intervals to all the Committees, and special literature supplied for local use when desired.

About March of this year it was decided to publish a black list of offending firms, both English and Irish. This list also contained the dumps whence Belfast goods were being distributed under cover. This list was widely circulated, and had the effect of bringing many of the offenders into line. A second and more comprehensive list was issued in May. Local black lists were printed at the request of the committees in several towns.

A very vigorous campaign against the Belfast, Ulster, and Northern Banks was initiated in June, and an order issued and prominently displayed in Dublin and the provinces declaring notes and cheques on these Banks illegal. The principal traders in Dublin were notified not to accept these notes in payment. Lists of persons having their accounts in these Banks were procured, and those concerned notified to withdraw such without delay. Evidence has come to hand that this campaign is one of the most potent of the boycott weapons.

There are some weak points in the boycott organisation. One is that, owing to the difficulties of forming Committees in the Counties of Antrim, Down, and Derry, we suspect that some towns in these areas are used for distributing Belfast goods. We have discovered several isolated cases of such camouflage and stopped them. We cannot, however, always tell whether goods sent out from these towns are bona fide or camouflaged Belfast goods. Owing to this difficulty, some committees have, on their own initiative, boycotted the whole six counties, and have been urging us to do the same. We also hear that in north-west Connaught, due partly to the arrest of the two organisers sent in succession, there is some leakage of Belfast goods.

Nor is the boycott of the Banks as complete as it should be. We are, however, hoping for an improvement in that district shortly, as we have sent out a third organiser who hopes to have committees functioning in most of the towns of Galway and Mayo before the end of the Truce.

The Labour Department has also been doing the executive work in connection with the British boycott. Generally speaking, shopkeepers and consumers are aiding loyally by the Prohibitions issued from time to time by Dáil Éireann. The piecemeal nature of the boycott, however, militates to some extent against successful drastic action. However, with the development of the boycott a more effective execution of the boycott may soon be expected. The Belfast boycott organisation is also working the British boycott.

Boycott Finances. The actual cost of running the Belfast and British boycotts between the 1st February and 31st July 1921, amounted to £5,450. The fines recovered (and paid into the Financial Department) during that period amounted to £400.

A pamphlet of 12,000 words giving the history of the 1920 and 1921 Belfast Pogroms has been prepared and will be submitted to the Publicity Department for publication.

Decree. It is hereby decreed that the Minister responsible for the carrying out of the Belfast and British Boycotts is empowered to inflict fines on firms and individuals who break, evade, or seek to evade these boycotts. There shall be no appeal to any other Department against the payment of these fines.

It was claimed that it was almost impossible for a Belfast merchant to sell a penny's worth of goods in the southern part of Ireland. Evidence that the boycott was having a serious impact on businesses in the designated areas is contained in one of a series of confidential RIC inspectors' reports of May 1921.[2] It reported 'the Belfast Boycott was spreading and extending to Ulster banks. It is useless to pretend that it is not extremely serious and it is significant to note that large English firms are now yielding to it and promising to obey the wishes of Dáil Éireann.'

The IRA was involved in a major campaign to disrupt the distribution of goods from the north of Ireland and roads were constantly blocked, vehicles attacked and their contents destroyed. Attacks were not just confined to the road network but also affected the railway, which was then the main method of goods transportation. An example of one such attack took place on 23 April 1921. The night goods and mail train from Belfast to Cavan, making its usual journey through Portadown and Armagh towards Clones and then Cavan, was held up after it had passed through the small station at Glasslough. At 2.40 a.m. it was signalled to stop by a large group of armed men. There was no way that the train could continue, as rails had been displaced further down the track – had the train continued it would have derailed. The driver, the fireman, the guard and the man in charge of the mail van next to the engine were ordered off the train and held at gunpoint. Mailbags were removed from the mail van while petrol was poured over the forty-two wagons that made up the train. The wagons were set on fire and as the fire started to take hold, the fireman was ordered to set the railway engine's controls to reverse and the engine restarted. The unmanned train, with the wagons now ablaze, reversed towards Glasslough. When the engine, with low steam pressure, eventually stopped on an incline, twenty-two wagons had been completely gutted.[3]

The boycott was eventually withdrawn following the Anglo-Irish Treaty, which was signed in the early hours of the morning on 6 December 1921. Michael Collins, now chairman of the Provisional Government of the Irish Free State, at a meeting with Sir James Craig on 21 January 1922, agreed that the boycott would be discontinued with immediate effect. The boycott, not unsurprisingly, was extremely unpopular in the unionist community and even after it had been withdrawn, *Newsletter* readers were provided with a list of products from southern Ireland and encouraged 'not to give a penny to the men who are endeavouring to crush you'.[4]

The deal reached between Collins and Craig was based on the understanding that Catholic workers would be facilitated in returning to work in the shipyards and the other firms from which they had been dismissed. Events in the newly formed state of Northern Ireland would make that an impossibility, as inter-communal warfare erupted in Belfast again following the shooting of special constables on a train at Clones railway station in County Monaghan on 11 February 1922.

21

Major Osbert Smyth versus Dan Breen

A world away from the ongoing war in Ireland a similar scenario was being played out in Egypt. Britain had invaded and occupied that country in 1882 on the pretext of restoring stability to the country, but commercial interests were the real reasons for Britain remaining as an occupying force. Cheap Egyptian cotton to supply British textile mills and control over the Suez Canal as the shortest route to India and the Far East dictated British policy in Egypt. Just as in Ireland, a growing nationalist movement, seeking self-government and an end to British occupation, had been placed on hold at the outbreak of the First World War. At the end of the war there was growing resentment of the British, fuelled by the way the country and its people had been treated during the war, which culminated in a violent revolt. In many ways it was a mirror image of what was taking place in Ireland.

Among the British soldiers sent to Egypt after the First World War was Major George Osbert Sterling Smyth, DSO, MC. He was posted as a Brigade Major with the 33rd Brigade, Royal Field Artillery. Major Smyth, at thirty years of age, was Colonel Smyth's young brother and was serving in Egypt when his brother was shot in the county club in Cork. He had been unable to return home in time to attend his brother's funeral.

Born on 27 January 1890 at Karpurthala in the Punjab, India, he had been educated at Campbell College, Belfast, before receiving private tuition, as did his brother, with Mr W.T. Kirkpatrick. He became a proficient linguist and was an interpreter of Hindustani,

Persian and French. Following in his brother's footsteps he also chose a military career and was commissioned from the Royal Military Academy, Woolwich, in 1907. He was wounded a number of times during the war. Major Smyth had, like his brother, a distinguished war record. He had been awarded the DSO, MC, Croix de Guerre, (French) and been mentioned in despatches five times.

The murder of his brother Gerald deeply affected Osbert and he was frustrated by the fact that he was thousands of miles away from the conflict in Ireland that had now become personal to him.

His brother's murder was of course only one of an increasing number of attacks on military and RIC personnel in Ireland at this time. British intelligence operating from Dublin Castle was failing to make any significant inroads into identifying the perpetrators and was proving to be no match for Michael Collins and his 'Squad', an elite group of undercover IRA men who reported directly to Collins. British intelligence operations were not properly structured and were uncoordinated. There was a need for a radical shake up and for experienced secret service agents. A number of such individuals were based in Cairo and they received orders to go to Ireland and to go undercover in Dublin.

When Osbert Smyth learned that intelligence officers were being transferred from Egypt to Ireland he immediately volunteered his services. He requested, and was granted, a posting to the intelligence service in Ireland. His objective was to avenge his brother's murder. He sailed from Alexandria on 30 July 1920 and arrived in Folkstone on 10 August. From there he made his way to Dublin and on to Banbridge. He arrived home on Sunday 15 August.[1] Having spent some time at the family home in Banbridge, helping to tidy up his brother's affairs and dealing with the many letters of condolences, he made his way to Dublin Castle to join an elite group of British intelligence officers. Along with eleven hand-picked men he joined a group that became known as the 'Cairo Gang' or the 'Murder Gang'. The leaders of the IRA were well known to military intelligence in Ireland and this group was given the task of tracking down and arresting or killing these individuals. It was not long, of course, before these intelligence officers became known to the IRA. Major Smyth, despite dressing in working-class clothes like the others, to blend in with the local population, stood out because of his height. His military records show that he was 6 foot 9½ inches tall.[2]

Michael Collins' Squad had been spectacularly successful in eliminating the 'political police' who were a threat to the IRA and he was aided in this by spies in Dublin Castle who had access to confidential information relating to intelligence matters. It was not until General Sir Ormonde Winter was appointed as head of British intelligence operations in Ireland that things changed. Among those specifically targeted was Dan Breen, the maverick Tipperary man, who had been responsible for killing the two policemen at Soloheadbeg on 21 January 1919. This incident – a bid to obtain explosives – is claimed to have triggered the start of the War of Independence/the Anglo-Irish war. This claim was encouraged by Breen, who was not known for his modesty. He was later listed as one of the 'most wanted' men, with a reward of £1,000 for information leading to his arrest. It was incorrectly assumed by the British that he had been responsible for the murder of Colonel Smyth in the county club in Cork and the full resources of British intelligence in Ireland were dedicated to finding and dealing with Breen.

In his account of events at that time, Breen recalled how in October 1920 he was 'on the run' from his native Tipperary and living in safe houses in Dublin. On a Friday night he was making his way from the Henry Street corner of Nelson's Pillar in the centre of Dublin to the home of Professor Carolan in Drumcondra. It was just after 11 p.m. and the trams were full of people making their way home before the midnight curfew. He had been spotted earlier by military intelligence officers and as he boarded the Whitehall tram bound for Drumcondra and made his way to the top deck, five men jumped on the tram and also made their way upstairs. Breen, always looking over his shoulder, recognised two of the men as members of the Cairo Gang. As Breen sat down so did they, one on each side of him. Another stood and two others made their way to the front of the tram. Breen had a choice: try to escape, or remain calm and await a move by his followers, if indeed they were following him. He opened a packet of cigarettes and lit one. As the tram entered Dorset Street he saw his travelling companions move their right hands to their hip pockets. According to Breen he produced his gun first and the two men sitting and the other one standing quickly left the tram. He followed them into the street. Both parties were reluctant to open fire in the crowded street and Breen made his escape down St Joseph's Terrace, only to double back and jump on the platform of a passing tram. He made his way to another safe house, that of the Fleming family from Tipperary, who lived above their grocer's shop in Drumcondra.

It was not long however before Major Smyth and his team caught up with him again. On the afternoon of 11 October Breen and fellow IRA man Seán Treacy went to the newly opened La Scala theatre on O'Connell Street to watch a film. As they left the cinema after the performance, Breen spotted one of the men who had sat beside him on the tram a few nights previously. Along with Treacy and three female acquaintances whom they had met as they left the cinema, he walked the short distance to Nelson's Pillar to catch a tram. As they boarded the tram one of the girls whispered to Breen that they were being followed. Breen, as he stepped on to the platform, turned around quickly and stared at the man who had been following them. The man did not join Breen and Treacy on the tram ride to Drumcondra and Fleming's safe house.

Aware that the net was closing, Treacy and Breen decided to leave Fleming's and go to Professor John Carolan's house, Fernside, on the main road to Belfast. Professor Carolan was employed at the nearby St Patrick's teacher training college and kept lodgers. Arriving about 11.30 p.m. and with the house in darkness, they let themselves in with a key that had been provided sometime previously and made their way to a top-floor bedroom that had been set aside for their use. At around 1 a.m. they were woken by the sound of men marching and the bright light of a searchlight trained on their window. When they heard the smashing of glass downstairs and the sound of footsteps on the stairs they knew that it was a raid and that the net had finally closed around them.

The raiding party was led by Major Smyth, Captain White and Captain Jeune. Major Smyth was not aware that Breen, one of the most wanted men in Ireland and the man he felt sure had murdered his brother, was in the house. For him and his colleagues this was just another raid on a house regarded as a safe house by the IRA. The raiding party had earlier that night been to Kingstown (Dún Laoghaire) to conduct a raid on a house there but had found nothing. They had then travelled north through Dublin to Drumcondra on the northern outskirts of the city to check out the home of Professor Carolan. Captain Robert D. Jeune, a member of the raiding party, along with officer Phil Attwood, took up position at the rear of the house while their colleagues gained entrance at the front.[3]

They began a systematic search of the house. Captain White and another soldier went upstairs to the second floor, where Mrs Carolan remained in bed as the room was checked. In a front bedroom they found an elderly man in bed: the startled man woken from his sleep told them that his name was Enright and that he was a former excise officer. As the room was being searched, Captain White saw Major Smyth open the next bedroom door, which was followed by a burst of gunfire from the room. Major Smyth was hit and fell to the floor. Captain White's colleague later recalled at the inquest how he and White had rushed to the door. Captain White got there first and was also shot. Dan Breen recounts a slightly different version of the shooting. He claimed that shots were fired through the closed bedroom door into the room he and Treacy had been sleeping in and he returned fire with his Mauser pistols. (This version would appear to be incorrect if Captain Jeune's account that this was just a speculative raid is to be believed). With bullets flying in both directions, Breen continued to fire into the landing and stairs. There was a thud, the sound of a man falling, and the shooting ceased for a few moments. His right hand injured, Breen used the brief lull to move to the landing, only to be faced with half a dozen soldiers armed with rifles coming up the stairs. He fired at the advancing soldiers and returned to his room, tripping over two dead bodies and a wounded soldier.[4] The bodies were those of Major Smyth and Captain White, the seriously wounded soldier was Corporal Worth.[5] Major Smyth had been hit twice in the chest, with one bullet going through his liver and the other through his right lung, striking his vertebra.[6] The bodies of the two dead officers were later taken to the King George V Military hospital.

As Breen went to escape through the window, shots were fired at him by a soldier who was covering the back of the house. Jeune and Attwood, on hearing the first shots, had rushed into the house, something Jeune later regarded as a grievous mistake. Wounded in five or six places and against all odds, Breen escaped. He sought help in a nearby house, selected at random, and was taken in and had his wounds attended to. He was later taken to the Mater hospital in Dublin and admitted under a false name. Despite a police and military raid on the hospital on 14 October Breen was not discovered. Treacy had also managed to escape early on in the confusion, only to be killed a few days later, on 14 October, when the military raided an IRA meeting at the Republican Outfitters drapery shop in Talbot Street.[7]

Professor Carolan had also been shot by the raiding party. His wife, who had locked herself and her children in her bedroom when the shooting started, ventured out only to find her husband seriously wounded. He was also taken, in critical condition, to the Mater hospital. While in hospital he made a statement that he had been shot in cold blood by one of the raiding party. He died a short time later from his wounds. The military version of what happened to Professor Carolan was somewhat different. When Major Smyth and Captain White were killed Professor Carolan was taken as a human shield and ordered to move ahead of the soldiers as they approached the room from which the shots had come. It was later claimed at the inquest into the shootings that Professor Carolan, as he got to the door of the room, turned, and was hit by a shot coming through the door. It was admitted that, 'under threats', Carolan had given Breen and Lacey [sic] the room to oblige a grocer named Fleming.[8] This version of events places the blame for the death of Professor Carolan on Breen and not on the military, as Carolan claimed as he lay dying in hospital. However, Captain Jeune, in writing many years later about this incident, which he regarded as a disastrous raid, admitted that Professor Carolan had 'been shot by mistake while being questioned'. It was 5.30 a.m. when the raiding party eventually left the house.

The Cairo Gang had stumbled on Breen and Treacy by accident and had paid a high price without capturing the most wanted man in Ireland. As far as the IRA were concerned this was evidence that the British intelligence network was starting to function and it would only be a matter of time before Michael Collins and Dan Breen were cornered. So concerned was Collins that he decided to launch a pre-emptive strike. His equally effective intelligence network had been able to identify many of the Cairo Gang and other intelligence officers. He was in possession of a posed photograph of some of the gang with their names written on the back. It had been relatively easy to identify some of these individuals, as they often left their suburban lodgings during curfew hours. Servants working in these houses noted this and passed the information to the IRA. On Sunday 21 November, in a series of simultaneous raids, Michael Collin's Squad assassinated thirteen British intelligence officers and two Auxiliary policemen.

Captain Jeune, who had accompanied Major Smyth on the fateful raid on Professor Carolan's house, was one of the few intelligence officers to survive. On that Saturday evening he was engaged in a search of the railway yards at Inchicore, Dublin where it was suspected that ammunition was being stored. When they drew a blank he and the other members of the search team decided to settle down for the night in a railway carriage. When he returned to his lodgings at 28 Upper Pembroke Street the following morning it was to a scene of carnage. Major C.M.G. Dowling, who was to relieve him that morning, was lying dead on the floor. In the doorway of the bathroom was the body of Captain Leonard Price. Colonel Woodcock had been shot three times, but later recovered. Captain Keenleyside had also been shot but survived. Colonel Hugh F. Montgomery, along with Major W. Woodcock had been shot. Woodcock survived but Colonel Montgomery later died of his wounds.

That afternoon there was a GAA football match between Dublin and Tipperary at Croke Park in Dublin. The police reckoned that IRA men, especially from Tipperary, would find it difficult to resist attending the match. They planned to seal off all the exit points and to stop and search individuals as they left the grounds after the match. There is considerable controversy as to what exactly happened when the mixed force of police, Auxiliaries and military arrived at Croke Park. It was claimed, in a subsequent military inquiry, held in camera, that spectators in the crowd shot at the police and fire was returned. People attending the match were adamant that the Auxiliaries were the first to fire and that they fired indiscriminately into the crowd. What is indisputable is that thirteen spectators were shot dead and many others injured. Michael Hogan, a Tipperary player, was riddled with bullets and died later in hospital. Documents recently made available by the Public Record Office show that 228 round of small arms were fired by the police and Auxiliaries and fifty rounds from an army machine gun.[9] Accounts of the length of time the shooting continued varies from ten to twenty minutes. However, Constance Markievicz, who had played a key part in the 1916 Easter Rising and was in Mountjoy jail at the time of the shooting, could hear the shooting: 'The Croke Park affair lasted 40 minutes by my watch and there were machine guns going, it felt like being back in the middle of Easter week. Croke Park is quite close. It's a miracle that so few were killed.'[10]

This action was seen by many as retaliation for the murder earlier that morning of the intelligence agents. The evidence collected at the military inquiry is contradictory and the question as to who fired the first shot on what came to be known as Bloody Sunday remains unanswered. A similar question would be asked fifty-two years later, in 1972, following another Bloody Sunday shooting involving the military and civilians.

This incident effectively brought to an end the activities of the Cairo Gang. Intelligence agents felt it was no longer safe to live in the community and sought refuge in Dublin Castle. The funeral of Major Smyth and Captain White took place on Thursday 14 October, with Smyth's remains being taken from the King George V Military hospital to Dublin's Amiens Street railway station (renamed Connolly Station in 1966) to be transported to Banbridge. Along the funeral route along the quays, members of Collins' Squad and British intelligence agents kept a wary eye on proceedings. The Squad had heard that the Chief Secretary for Ireland, Sir Hamar Greenwood, General Tudor and other prominent officials would take part in the funeral procession and had plans to assassinate them as the cortège made its way along the quays. However, none of the individuals targeted took part. Major Smyth's mother travelled to Dublin along with her brother Norman Ferguson and Mr and Mrs Murland and Warren Murland, cousins of the deceased. They accompanied the body on the journey back to Banbridge.

The remains arrived in Banbridge on the 5.30 p.m. train and the oak coffin was taken from the guard's van by six employees from Edenderry factory and carried to the waiting hearse. A wreath of white chrysanthemums, with a card on which was written 'With deepest sympathy from Colonels Ross and Hardy', was placed on the coffin. Major Smyth was then taken for the last time to Clonaslee House.

Major George Osbert Sterling Smyth, DSO, MC, who had led an effective intelligence operation against the IRA and who had died in the line of duty on 12 October, three months after his brother had been gunned down in Cork, was to be buried alongside his brother. The funeral from Clonaslee House, on Friday 15 October, was to follow the same route as his brother's three months earlier. The Duke of Cornwall's light infantry stood to attention as the coffin was removed from the house, following a short service by Rev. J. Kyle from Tullylish, and placed on a gun carriage drawn by two black chargers. For the second time, a mother placed a wreath on the coffin of a son. The laurel wreath with white lilies had the simple inscription 'To the most devoted and loving son that ever lived'. With guns reversed the military guard of honour preceded the gun carriage. Once again the Smyth and Ferguson families filed behind the coffin. Directly behind the gun carriage a sergeant walked with Major Smyth's faithful dog, a rough-coated terrier. The respective families were represented by

Howard Ferguson, Stanley Ferguson, Norman Ferguson, Captain Thomas Ferguson, James Ferguson and Thomas J. Ferguson. The Smyth family was represented by Dr Malcolm Smyth, David Smyth and Brice Smyth. The Murland family was also represented. Other mourners included Major General H.H. Tudor, Brigadier General Sir William Hacket Pain (Divisional Police Commander for the North of Ireland) and a detachment of the Dublin Military Police under Chief Commissioner Colonel Edgeworth Johnstone. The Royal Irish Constabulary was also well represented.

Practically all work ceased in Banbridge during the funeral and the route through the town to the cemetery was lined with sympathisers. The final service at the graveside was conducted by Rev. Charles Grierson, BD, Lord Bishop of Down, Connor and Dromore. Three volleys of shots were fired over the grave as a final salute and the 'Last Post' sounded. Major Smyth was to be the last of five members of the Smyths of Banbridge to lay down their lives in service to their country.

Major George Osbert Sterling Smyth's death did not lead to the violence in Banbridge and other towns that followed the funeral of his brother.

Divisional Commissioner Philip Holmes

Meanwhile in Cork, the killings continued and the murder of Colonel Smyth quickly became another statistic. He had been replaced as Divisional Commissioner by Philip A. Holmes, a native of Cork city. Holmes, like Colonel Smyth, was another senior ex-army officer figure, having achieved the rank of Brigadier General while serving with the Royal Irish Regiment during the First World War.

He had been a major in that regiment and had served in Dublin during the 1916 Easter Rising. He was subsequently a witness at the trial of Joseph Plunkett, one of the leaders of the rising. On 2 May 1916 in a trial conducted in camera, Joseph Plunkett was charged with taking part in the rebellion and 'the waging of war against His Majesty the King'. Holmes identified Plunkett as one of the leaders who had surrendered on the evening of 29 April. Plunkett was found guilty and an order was made that he should be executed by a firing squad. There is a rather poignant story attached to this. The afternoon following his trial, Plunkett's girlfriend, Grace Gifford, whom he intended to marry, made her way along Grafton Street in Dublin to a jeweller's shop. When she reached the shop it was about to close for the night. She persuaded the jeweller to delay closing and to allow her to buy a wedding ring.

On 4 May Grace was led into the small chapel in Kilmainham jail and by candlelight in the early hours of the morning, with Joseph Plunkett standing in handcuffs beside her, they were married. Following the ceremony, conducted by Rev. Eugene MacCarthy, Plunkett was led away. Before his execution later that morning he was allowed to see his new wife for ten minutes, timed by a soldier. An hour later he was taken to the yard in Kilmainham jail and executed by firing squad.

Divisional Commissioner Holmes was to meet the same fate as his predecessor. He was shot in an IRA ambush at Tureengarriff, near Castleisland on the Cork-Kerry border on 28 January 1921. The IRA had observed an army convoy travelling west and reckoned it would return on the same road. They set up an ambush and waited for two days for the vehicles to return. A trench was dug in the road to halt the vehicles. When the returning convoy arrived it was brought to a halt and the IRA opened fire. Despite the army officers returning fire, two RIC constables, Thomas Moyles and James Hoare, were shot dead. Three others were wounded. Divisional Commissioner Holmes was seriously injured. The army officers, realising that they were all about to be slaughtered, surrendered. The IRA started to search the prisoners and to tend to the wounded. Holmes knew that he had been fatally wounded and asked to be left alone, saying that he was finished. He asked for and was given a cigarette. A passing motorist coming from the Cork direction was stopped and asked to bring Holmes to the county infirmary in Tralee, where he died the following day.[11] He was forty-four years old. The convoy had been returning from Listowel, where Divisional Commissioner Holmes had been investigating the murder of District Inspector Tobias O'Sullivan, who had been shot on 20 January outside Listowel barracks.

22

The Arrests

Following the assassination of DI Swanzy the first person to be arrested was Seán Leonard. The registration number of the getaway car had been noted by a number of people, including the doctor's wife who had scratched the number on her windowsill in her upstairs bedroom. It had been traced to a garage at Upper Library Street in Belfast and Mr A.G. Apengis, the Greek owner of the firm, confirmed that Sean Leonard – who had been employed by him for about one year – had been the driver of the taxi at the time Swanzy was murdered.

Leonard, originally from Tourlestane, near Tubbercurry, County Sligo, was one of a family of ten, six girls and four boys. He had moved to Belfast around 1917 and had found work as a taxi driver. He was also a member of the IRA. At the time of his arrest he was living at Bedeque Street, Belfast. Arrested along with him were James Joseph Montgomery of Oldpark Road and his brother John Vincent Montgomery, 38 Rosepenna Street. They were arrested on 25 August and brought to the Central RIC barracks in Belfast. The police had the accused brought before the Recorder's Court, Townhall Street, Belfast on 3 September to appear before George McElroy, RM, and J. Quigley, JP. District Inspector McNally from Lisburn prosecuted. He informed the court that his investigations were not yet complete and asked for a remand until 11 September. Mr. Fox, representing the Montgomery brothers, thought it only fair in the interests of the men he represented, to say that their people had been threatened and intimidated since being arrested. McElroy responded saying that there were certain people in Belfast and Lisburn who had taken upon themselves the authority of the king's courts to judge others guilty of crimes and to punish them, which was altogether illegal, and the people who did this were disloyal to the king, no matter how much they professed their loyalty. It amounted to high treason and the sooner it was stopped the better.

John Tipping from Edward Street, Lurgan, was arrested next by the Lurgan police on 6 September and was charged with being involved in the murder of DI Swanzy.

The accused were remanded until 11 September and then there were further remands to 17 and then 24 September. At the end of November a writ of *habeas corpus* was sought in the King's Bench division in Dublin on the grounds that they had been in jail for three and a half months without any evidence presented against them and without facing a trial. The following day the Montgomery brothers were released without charge.

Leonard appeared before a court-martial at Victoria barracks, Belfast, and was represented by T.M. Healy, J. Campbell and James McSparran (instructed by Messers Donnelly & Co). Timothy Healy, a barrister and a former member of parliament for South Derry, later became the first Governor-General in the Irish Free State. In a letter to his brother about the affair, which contains a number of inaccuracies, he wrote:

The murder in Lisburn, in the heart of Orangeism, is the more daring than anything that has taken place. Swanzy is accused of having organised your Lord Mayor MacCurtain's murder. The Wexford District Inspector (an Englishman who used to drink) was shot because, it is said, he fired first at the Lord Mayor. Someone in the Four Courts told me that the police party who were brigaded to kill the Lord Mayor consisted of 14, and that the Sinn Féiners have their names, and intend to kill all of them. This is terrible, but explains many of the deaths of policemen scattered through the country, as they were removed from

Cork, or were not stationed there. I defended, at a court-martial in Belfast, the chauffeur who was charged with driving the party which shot Swanzy. He was convicted, but I wrote to General Macready that an Orange jury would not have found him guilty, and he was reprieved … General Macready, however, with merciful prudence recommended the Viceroy, Lord French, to reprieve Leonard. As a rule, courts-martial composed of officer of the British Army make a fine tribunal. Some of the Belfast officers accompanied me nightly on my walk to my hotel (unasked) after I had pleaded before them on behalf of Sinn Féiners, lest Orange wrath should fall on me.

It must be assumed that Healy made the case at the court-martial that Leonard was an innocent individual and compared him to George Nelson, the Protestant taxi driver who was forced to co-operate during the previous attempt to murder Swanzy. Leonard claimed that he had been held at gunpoint, as was Nelson, while the attack took place. The trial concluded on 3 February 1921, following a visit by members of the court to Lisburn to see at first hand the scene of the murder. After what had been a lengthy trial, there was some doubt as to whether he was one of the men actually involved in the shooting or not. The court found Leonard not guilty of the charge of manslaughter. The decision in the charge of murder was to be made known to the public 'in the usual way'. Following his release Leonard returned to Sligo, where he later started up a motor business in Collooney, County Sligo.

John Cusack, 7 Little York Street, was also suspected of being involved in the murder of DI Swanzy but was not arrested. Cusack, a close friend of Joe McKelvey who had staked out Swanzy before his murder, was an intelligence officer in the Belfast IRA. In a report written by RIC Commissioner J.F. Gelston, he noted that Cusack was 'a prominent IRA man and also an IRB man. He was without doubt Collins' right hand man during the murders in Ireland and information of which I have little doubt was received that he planned the murder of Mr. Swanzy in Lisburn … This is a dangerous man, a perfect organiser and would be a menace to the peace of the city'.[1]

23

Compensation Claims

Judge Matheson heard the claims for compensation following the August riots in 1921 in the county courthouse in Belfast. Lisburn Urban Council was represented by K.C. Best. Lisburn Rural Council was represented by J. Lowry and Antrim County Council was represented by T.W. Brown, while R.J. Dick represented Down Council.

Individual householders who had furniture and personal belonging taken from their houses and stolen or burned, and individuals who had their homes burned and were left homeless, appeared in a court for the first time in their lives. The solicitors representing the various councils were intent from the outset on reducing the cost of the compensation claims to the councils as much as possible. They had little interest in the impact the destruction had on individuals and their lives. They approached the compensation claims on the basis that they had been inflated by fifty per cent and this was generally reflected in the subsequent awards made. The hearings were a source of amusement to the solicitors, who played to the gallery in challenging and ridiculing claims.

Typical of the cross-examination of the claimants was that of Hugh Gorman of Clonard Gardens, Belfast, who had claimed £50 in respect of property destroyed at his father-in-law's shop at 23 Bridge Street. When he said that he was employed as an engineer but had helped out by serving in the shop, he was mockingly asked if his job was to put the little hard nuts in the sweets – and did he make the paper bags? When he confirmed that he did make paper bags, Mr Brown drew laughter from the court in repeating that here was an engineer making paper bags.

Thomas Carson claimed £1,100 for the destruction of stock and furniture at his confectionery shop at 31 Bow Street on 22 August. Brown, commenting on the number of claims from Bow Street for sweet shops, said that the people must have lived on caramels and chocolates if he was to believe the stories of the large stocks kept in the shops. He was awarded £380.

Every item for which compensation was claimed was examined in detail by solicitors acting for the councils. In some cases they refused to accept that private houses had the furniture claimed for. In one case the solicitor said it was physically impossible for the house to have contained the furniture, especially a piano which was stolen. He pointed out that the kitchen house was only 9 foot 6 inches wide, with an extra 18 inches over a gateway. The judge, however, having listened to the evidence, said that it was clear that the best part of the furniture – including the piano – had been removed, and gave a decree for £100.

The solicitors were eventually successful in reducing the initial compensation claim for £806,538 to £233,952. Lisburn Urban Council awarded fire chief William Megran £40 for his exceptional service during the riots and some of the volunteer firemen also received monetary awards. A sum of £49.17s was allocated to the Belfast fire brigade for attending. (Their efforts in trying to put out the many fires had been hampered to such an extent that they had given up and returned to base.)

It came as quite a shock to the loyalist ratepayers in Lisburn that, while there might have been a certain unwillingness by the police and the military under the direction of Sir Hacket Pain to prevent the destruction of property, the judiciary was not prepared to turn a blind eye when it came to reparation for the damage done. Justice Matheson took a firm line regarding responsibility for the payment of compensation. In the cold light of day the reality was that the community that had caused the destruction was going to have to pay the compensation. In a test case, Justice Matheson said: 'It was purely a local crime or a series of crimes and did not know why any other locality, except that in which the crimes were committed should pay toll for it.' He went on to say that as far as he was concerned he regarded the affair as pure blackguardism and why the blackguardism of Lisburn should be paid for by anyone else he failed to see. He said that the stories that had been told before him represented the most shocking state of things he had ever heard of. No distinction between rich and poor was made; there were poor people struggling in Lisburn and there were men, who, through their own industry, had acquired substantial fortunes, and all were treated alike. The judge's decision was that the urban district of Lisburn and the rural district of Lisburn should bear the burden of the charge according to their respective valuations.[1]

In March 1921 the Right Honourable Justice Dodd heard an appeal regarding the claim for compensation submitted on behalf of DI Swanzy's mother Elizabeth and her daughter Irene. An initial claim for £15,000 had been made, but the claim presented to the court that March day was for £4,500. The case was made to the judge that had Swanzy lived and remained in the RIC he would have had an annual pension of £600. A sympathetic Justice Dodd said that the deceased had 'put his shoulder to the wheel' in restoring the family fortune and decided that the claim submitted by Mrs Swanzy's solicitor was too modest. He increased the compensation to £6,000. Judge Matheson had originally decreed that Lisburn Urban and Rural District Councils should bear the cost, but Justice Dodd decided that the compensation was to be levied over portions of County Antrim, County Down and the Lisburn area. This decision by Judge Dodd to vary the ruling made by Judge Matheson caused some confusion and it was not long until the solicitors, who had represented the various councils at the compensation hearing, started squabbling among themselves.

It was not long until the solicitors who had represented the various councils at the compensation hearings started squabbling among themselves. Mr Best, representing Lisburn, argued that the compensation bill should be divided equally between Counties Down and Antrim. (The River Lagan divides Lisburn between the two counties.) Mr Andrews, representing Down Council felt that that would be a grave injustice, as Down would have to pay the larger part for a crime committed in County Antrim.

It was a sobering thought for the ratepayers that having seen their town centre destroyed, with hundreds unemployed as a result of the damage to shops and businesses, they were now to be faced with a substantial rise in their rates for years to come. Lisburn Urban Council felt it had little option but to accept the court's ruling and bear the cost. The outcry among the ratepayers was such that a public meeting was called and the outcome was the establishment of the Lisburn Ratepayers' Association under the chairmanship of J.G. Hanna. A deputation from the association urged the council to cut spending wherever possible to reduce the rate burden. At the same time an appeal against Judge Matheson's ruling was lodged.

In August 1921 Judge Samuels, sitting in the courthouse in Belfast, heard the appeal. He detailed the compensation for damage done during the July riots and the burning and looting in August and September. During this period a total of 278 houses or other premises were burned out and there was immense damaged done to furniture, goods and merchandise.[2]

Justice Samuel's ruling was that the compensation costs were to be spread over a wider area, including Belfast rural district. The amount awarded as compensation was apportioned as one-third on Lisburn Urban District Council, one-third on Lisburn Rural District Council, plus the electoral divisions of Crumlin and Dundesert in the Antrim rural district and Ballygomartain in the Belfast rural district and the final one-third from the Hillsborough and Moira rural districts. Justice Samuels, in explaining the decision to spread the burden of compensation for damage done over such an extensive area, stated that he had received much evidence 'that the local Lisburn rioters were accompanied and aided by numbers of strangers from the country districts and that plunder was carted away to the north and south of the town'. He maintained that this continued 'holocaust' was not merely the work of Lisburn people but instead, the desire for revenge became epidemic and affected the population of a much wider district. The riots drew troublemakers into the town from the surrounding areas, especially people who were able to reach Lisburn and return to their homes within a few hours.

Justice Samuel's verdict immediately provoked resentment, particularly in the rural areas of Lisburn which were now being forced to bear part of the cost. A meeting of Hillsborough ratepayers passed a resolution claiming that the amount levied on the rural district of Hillsborough should be borne by the state. It was their opinion that the protection to which the taxpayer was entitled was not provided by the police or military and that 'owing to the negligence or indifference displayed by the forces of the town, the burnings continued for days'. The people of Aghalee, who had just recently been brought under the control of Lisburn Rural District Council also protested against having to bear part of the cost, claiming that they had no share in 'the burnings'. Lisburn Rural District Council also denied having any responsibility.

The Lisburn Farmers' Association held a meeting and passed a resolution demanding a government grant to meet the awards 'as it was owing to the lack of protection by the police and military authorities that the damage was done'. They maintained that the rate-payer was already overburdened and to reduce the rate they proposed an end to the practice of direct labour on the roads, all public works to be carried out by competitive contracts, the end of war-time salaries being paid to officials, and greater supervision over gangs of men engaged on the roads. The bulk of the cost fell to the Lisburn ratepayers. Rates rose from 9s 3d for the 1918-19 financial year to 13s 10d and to £1 1s 4d in 1921-22. With almost a three-fold increase in the rates over three years, this was an enormous burden for the Lisburn ratepayer, especially at a time of falling wages and an economic recession.[3]

The legal wrangling continued and it was finally agreed that the new government for Northern Ireland, which had been established in June 1921, would meet the full compensation costs, and grants were allocated to the relevant district councils. The ratepayers and those engaged in looting, arson and the destruction of Lisburn, were off the hook

24

Nothing Changes

In March 1921, six months after the riots that had left Lisburn in ruins had finally eased, the sectarianism, which had led to such widespread destruction, once again manifested itself. Following the end of the First World War, Ex-Servicemen's Associations had been formed in Britain's towns and cities. War-time Prime Minister Lloyd George had promised the soldiers who had fought in the war that they would return to a land fit for heroes. Those who survived found that jobs for returning soldiers were few and far between and the government left them to fend for themselves. The Ex-Servicemen's Associations provided practical support to enable the former soldiers find work and re-integrate into society.

A meeting was organised in the Temperance Institute in Railway Street to start a local branch of the Ulster Ex-Servicemen's Association. Dr George St George, chairman of Lisburn Urban Council, chaired the meeting. He explained that the role of the association was to link loyalists in Ulster to form one united group of former soldiers, and its primary task was to help men to find employment. Ignoring the sacrifices made by the mainly nationalist 16th Division, which had fought and died alongside the loyalist 36th Division, he made it clear that it did not matter to him that Catholics had also fought and died for their country. It mattered little to him that Catholics also found themselves unemployed – they were to be excluded from the association. Dr St George justified this decision by saying that there were men who went to the front to train to become soldiers simply to be able to instruct Sinn Féin.

Robert Boyd, the organising secretary, went further by saying, 'we not only bar Sinn Féiners but we bar Red Flagers, Bolshevists all extreme socialists because we hold that there is not much difference when they come to be weighed in the balance'. H.T. Whitaker, a solicitor and member of the organising committee, played the fear factor card to unite his audience. He addressed the assembled former servicemen: 'You know at present there are three parties in Ireland, the Protestant loyal party – the Roman Catholic disloyal party which is one of the shrewdest and cleverest parties that you could ever find. There will be strong opposition to the Ulster Parliament and that opposition will consist of the Roman Catholic Party and the Labour Party because they will be banded together to vote in the South of Ireland. If the Protestants of Northern Ireland do not do their duty there will be only one Party in the Ulster Parliament and boys you all remember there is a day on the 12th July when we celebrate the glorious victory that King William won for us.' To rapturous applause he revealed the real purpose of the association – loyalist political muscle. 'You have a battalion here 800 strong with Dr St George at your head; there is no person in Lisburn (who) will refuse you anything'. Pressure was brought on employers in the Lisburn area again to employ only Protestant workers. An 800-strong group of loyalists with military experience had been created to be held in reserve. Coincidentally this was the same number of special constables in the Lisburn area.

So only months after the end of unprecedented violence against the Catholic community in Lisburn, the sectarian embers continued to smoulder. Civic leaders were once again threatening to use force to ensure loyalist domination in the town. It is important to note that their comments were directed at what would be regarded as loyalist employers – the unelected group were dictating discriminatory employment practices to local employers. They were secure in the knowledge that whatever action was taken to enforce their policy, it would not be opposed. They knew that the police would not and now could not take any action. They knew that few employers would be prepared to face the prospect of crowds supported by Orange Order bands protesting outside their factories. A template for the future had been established.

Notes

Preface
1. T. Ryle Dwyer, *Tans, Terror and Troubles*, Cork: Mercier Press 2001.
2. Michael Farrell, *Northern Ireland, The Orange State*, London: Pluto Press 1980.

2   The Murder of Tomás MacCurtain in Cork
1. PRONI MIC/448/72.
2. John Borgonovo, *Florence and Josephine O'Donoghue's War of Independence*, Dublin & Portland, Oregon: Irish Academic Press 2006, p.69.
3. Ibid., p.89.
4. Ibid., p.52.
5. R. Abbott, *Police Casualties in Ireland 1919-1922*, Cork: Mercier Press 2000.
6. John Borgonovo, *op. cit.*, p.48.
7. Peter Hart, *The IRA and its Enemies: Violence and Community in Cork 1916-1923*, Oxford: Oxford University Press 1998.
8. Alan F. Parkinson in his book *Belfast's Unholy War*, Dublin: Four Courts Press 2004 p.28, claims that Colonel Smyth was involved in the murder of Tomás MacCurtain. Smyth was not named at the inquest and had not been appointed as Divisional Police Commissioner for Munster in March when the murder took place.
9. *Daily Mail*, special correspondence Dublin, 22 March 1920.
10. Fionnuala MacCurtain, *Remember it's for Ireland*, Cork: Mercier Press 2007, p.137.
11. Peter Hart, *op. cit.*, p.10.
12. Fionnuala MacCurtain, *op cit.*, p.160.
13. Dan Breen, *My Fight for Irish Freedom*, Dublin: The Talbot Press 1955.

3   Swanzy leaves Cork
1. R. Abbott, *op. cit.*
2. John Borgonovo, *op. cit.*, p.71.
3. O'Malley Papers P17b/108.
4. *Lisburn Standard*, August 1920.

4   The Listowel Mutiny
1. An account by Jeremiah Mee in the *Cork Examiner*, 25 January 1922.
2. W. Haughton Crowe, *Bridges to Banbridge*.
3. Paul McCandless, *Smyths of the Bann*, Banbridge 2002.
4. Howard Ferguson, *Murland Dairies*, courtesy of Jerry Murland 2007.
5. Ibid.
6. Ibid.
7. T. Ryle Dwyer, *Tans, Terror and Troubles*, Cork: Mercier Press 2001.

8. Lawrence James, *Raj – The making of British India,* London: Abacus 2007 p.473.
9. A.N. Wilson, *After the Victorians,* London: Random House 2002 p.209.
10. Lawrence James, *op. cit.* p.480.
11. Hansard 8 July 1920.
12. R. Abbott, *op cit.*
13. Reported in the *Daily Mail.*
14. J. Anthony Gaughan, *Memories of Constable Jeremiah Mee RIC,* Dublin: Anvil Books 1975.
15. Brig.-General G. Walker, *Memoir Bt. Lieut-Colonel Gerald B. F. Smyth, D. S. O. Royal Engineers,* London: The Royal Engineers Journal Oct 1920.
16. Dáil Éireann vol. 2, August 1921.

5   The murder of Colonel Smyth
1. J. Anthony Gaughan, *op. cit.*

6   Colonel Smyth's Funeral
1. *Belfast Telegraph,* 21 July 1920.

7   Banbridge Riots
1. *The Troubles – A history of the Northern Ireland conflict*, Glenravel publications.
2. *The Down Recorder,* 5 June 1920.
3. *Banbridge Chronicle,* 24 July 1920.
4. *The Frontier Sentinel,* 9 October 1920.
5. A. Dillon, *Memories of Banbridge resident.*
6. *Banbridge Chronicle,* 21 Aug 1920.
7. *Irish Bulletin*, Vol. 5, No. 37, 2 September 1921.
8. *Northern Whig,* 10 May 1927.

8   Dromore Riots
1. *Banbridge Chronicle,* 7 August 1920.
2. *Newsletter,* 27 July 1920.

9   Lisburn Riots
1. Rev. Ambrose Macaulay, *Convent of the Sacred Heart of Mary – Survey of a Century 1870-1970.*
2. PRONI MIC/448/72 County Inspector's Report Co. Down July 1920.

10 Violence spreads
1. Jonathan Bardon, *Belfast: An Illustrated History*, Belfast: Blackstaff Press 1982 p.191.
2. *Lisburn Standard.*
3. A.T.O. Stewart, *The Ulster Crisis: Resistance to Home Rule, 1912-1914.* Belfast: Blackstaff Press 1997, pp.62-63.
4. *Lisburn Standard.*
5. G.B. Kenna, *Facts and Figures Belfast Progrom 1920-1922*, Dublin: The O'Connell Publishing Company 1922, p.18.

6. Jonathan Bardon, *A History of Ulster*, Belfast: Blackstaff Press 1992, p.471.

12 Planning to murder Swanzy

1. *The Down Recorder*, 26 August 1920.
2. T. Ryle Dwyer, *The Squad*, Cork: Mercier Press 2000 p.120.
3. Jim McDermott, *Northern Divisions The Old IRA and the Belfast Pogroms 1920–1922*, Belfast: BTP Publications 2001, p.50.
4. John Borgonovo, *op. cit*. p.136.
5. Initially three men from Cork – Culhane, O'Donovan and Cody – travelled north to assassinate Swanzy in Lisburn. Culhane later returned with Dick Murphy.

13 The Murder of District Inspector Swanzy

1. T. Ryle Dwyer, *The Squad*, p.122.
2. Hugh Bass, *Records and Recollections of Alexander Boyd & Co. Ltd., Castle Street Lisburn*, Belfast : Nicholson & Bass Ltd. 1977.

14 The Burning of Lisburn

1. *Belfast Telegraph*, 28 August.
2. *Northern Whig*, 24 August 1920.
3. Cahal Bradley, *History of St. Patrick's Lisburn*.
4. *Belfast Telegraph*, 24 August 1920.
5. A.T.Q. Stewart, *op cit*.
6. O'Mally Papers P17b 108.
7. Jim McDermott, *op. cit*.
8. O'Mally Papers P17b 108.
9. O'Mally Papers P17b 108.
10. Brian S. Turner, *Voices from the Street*, Lisburn City Centre Management 2007
11. *Irish News*, 2 April 1943. A report on the death of Canon O'Boyle makes reference to events in Lisburn in 1920.
12. Irish White Cross Society Reports 1922.
13. Rev. Ambrose Macaulay, *Survey of a Century 1870-1970*.
14. *Belfast Telegraph*, 24 August 1920.
15. Jonathan Bardon, *A History of Ulster*, Belfast: Blackstaff Press 1992.
16. Recollection by a survivor.

15 No Regrets

1. Jim Herlihy, *The Royal Irish Constabulary: A Complete Alphabetical List of Officers and Men 1816-1922*, Dublin: Four Courts Press 1999.
2. Ian Colvin, *The Life of Lord Carson* Vol. 3, p.398.

16 Birth of the Ulster Special Constabulary

1. Jonathan Bardon, *A History of Ulster*, Belfast: Blackstaff Press 1992 p.475.
2. John Ainsworth, *Kevin Barry, the Incident at Monk's Bakery and the making of an Irish Republican*, Blackwell Publishers 2002.

3. Sturgis, Mark. (Hopkinson, Michael), *The Last Days of Dublin Castle: The Mark Sturgis Diaries*, Dublin: Irish Academic Press 1999 p.63.

17 The Lisburn Mutiny
1. PRONI FIN 18/1/73.
2. PRONI D/1022/12/1.
3. PRONI FIN 18/1/45.
4. Jim McDermott, *op. cit.*, p.57.

18 Dundalk Reprisals
1. *Belfast Telegraph,* 28 Aug 1920.

19 The District Inspector Ferris Incident
1. Alan Parkinson, *Belfast's Unholy War,* Dublin: Four Courts Press 2004 p.1160.
2. Jim McDermott, *op. cit.*, p.185.

20 Belfast Boycott
1. Jim McDermott, *op. cit.*, p.48.
2. MIC 448, PRONI.
3. PRONI RIC Report D/3465/3/37/139/3.
4. *Belfast Newsletter*, 20 May 1922.

21 Major Osbert Smyth versus Dan Breen
1. Howard Ferguson, *Murland Dairies*, courtesy of Jerry Murland 2007.
2. Paul McCandless, *op. cit.*
3. William Sheehan, *British Voices from the Irish War of Independence 1918-1921*, Cork: The Collins Press 2006 pp.87-8.
4. Dan Breen, *op. cit.*
5. Richard Abbott, *op. cit.*
6. Paul McCandless, *op. cit.*
7. Dan Breen, *op. cit.*
8. *Banbridge Chronicle,* 28 Oct. 1920.
9. File WO 35/88 Public Record Office Kew, London.
10. Jacqueline van Voris, *Constance de Markievicz – In the Cause of Ireland,* Amherst: The University of Massachusetts Press p.28.
11. T. Ryle Dwyer, *Tans, Terror and Troubles,* p.275.

22 The Arrests
1. PRONI HA/32/1/271.

23 Compensation Claims
1. *Lisburn Standard.*
2. *Lisburn Standard,* 5 August 1921.
3. Thesis by Gerald E. Kelly, February 1975.

Index